SIR GEORGE SOMERS
A Man And His Times

by
David F. Raine

POMPANO PUBLICATIONS
Bridge House Art Gallery
off King's Square
St. George's, Bermuda GE01

1st Edition 1984
2nd Edition 1985
3rd Edition 1986
4th Edition 1994

ISBN 0-921962-10-X

Other Books by the same author:

PITSEOLAK — A CANADIAN TRAGEDY
THE PREGNANT FATHER
ARCHITECTURE—BERMUDA STYLE
THE HISTORIC TOWNE OF ST. GEORGE
ANOTHER WORLD
APA POCKET GUIDE
RATTLE AND SHAKE
BERMUDA AS IT USED TO BE
SIR GEORGE SOMERS –A MAN AND HIS TIMES
THE IMPRISONED SPLENDOUR

Cover design by the author.

Table Of Contents

Wax sculpture of Sir George Somers, by Desmond Hale Fountain.

Preface

This book originally began as a single brief passage, to be included in another book which I was revising. However, the deeper that I delved into the life and accomplishments of this distinguished seaman, the more I began to appreciate that he really warranted something far more substantial than just a few casual words. This, the first complete biography of Sir George Somers, is the result.

It is at once remarkable to realise that George Somers was a Englishman who rose from relative obscurity to become the Mayor of Lyme Regis, the accredited Founder of Bermuda and also a Saviour of the fledgling colony of Virginia, in the United States. Such diverse claims to fame are indeed unique!

Research alone has taken the better part of two years and has involved exploring the archives of libraries, museums and private foundations. Documents held by the British, Bermudian, Canadian and American Governments have been examined, sifted and checked for even the slightest fact or references, which might have some bearing on the life and accomplishments of this one man. In addition to this, I have indulged in exhaustive correspondence with archivists and historians as far-flung as Washington, London and Mexico City.

I have also attempted to reconstruct some authentic real-life situations so that the reader may experience some of the emotions and background circumstances which had an effect on the events of his life. I consider these to be important ingredients in gaining a meaningful insight into Sir George Somers as a person. Therefore, during the course of actually writing the text itself I walked the streets of his childhood, fished where he did and stood in the grounds of his country manor. Sitting in the garden of eminent British novelist John Fowles, overlooking Lyme Regis, I enjoyed the same views and salty smells of the harbour which Sir George Somers loved so much. I have stood on the quayside steps where his dead body was eventually brought ashore; and I have felt the chill and silence of the small English village church in which his remains were finally interred.

Through the clear waters off Bermuda, I have peered down at the wreck of his "Sea Venture," still locked in the same coral reef on which it floundered in 1609. In Venezuela, I stood atop the same mountains from which he contemplated his attack against Caracas.

Throughout my research, I have tried to locate every available source which might provide clues and verifiable facts associated with his life. I have questioned accepted information and cross-checked traditional beliefs—referring to faded original parchments with such regularity that I found myself translating, with familiarity and ease, the curious speech and elegant writing of sixteenth century Elizabethan scribes.

In earnest I have sought the truth, because I feel that this is the commitment and obligation of all biographers.

Inevitably there are some instances of supposition, but these are always based upon the firmest and most solid pieces of circumstantial evidence. We must realise that complete, intimate records of each individual life have been the perogative of more-recent twentieth century "technology." Unfortunately, many of the finer points relating to individual backgrounds from 400 years ago simply do not exist.

But, even if every single desireable scrap of information about Sir George Somers was not always readily available, then there is some consolation to be taken from the fact that so much of the jigsaw of his life has now been assembled, with confidence and accuracy. Biographers of men such as Christopher Newport and John White, for example—both Englishmen, who were key figures in the colonization of Virginia—will be far more frustrated than I have been.

And if this book provokes scholarly discussion, or dissention; or if it witnesses the re-surfacing of some hitherto undiscovered information, then it will have also have accomplished another ultimate objective. For this, the first complete biography of Sir George Somers, is hopefully but the beginning . . .

David F. Raine,
St. David's Island,
Bermuda.

Acknowledgements

Throughout the preparation of this book, my own research has been greatly facilitated by the unfailing cooperation, patience and researches of others. They have responded to endless letters, telephone calls and visits, with courtesy; they have replied to my questions with tolerance and I have benefitted from their internationally respected opinions.

In particular, I wish to thank:

Susan Berg of the Colonial Williamsburg Foundation, in Virginia; James Flatness of the Library of Congress in Washington; the Chief Park Historian with the United States Department of the Interior; Edward H. Dahl of the Public Archives of Canada; A. W. H. Pearsall, Historian to the National Maritime Museum of England; staff at the Department of Manuscripts, in the British Museum—in particular Ms. F. Grisdale; Mrs. J. Hearn of the Dorset County Museum, England; the members of the Dorset Natural History and Archaeological Society—whose devotion has preserved a lot of vital history; Derek M. M. Shorrocks, Archivist to the Somerset County Council; Tony Campbell, Research Assistant at The British Library, in London; D. Crook of the Search Department at the Public Record Office, in London; John Fowles of Lyme Regis who so openly shared his own researches, as Curator of the town's museum; the diligent part-time staff at the Philpott Museum in Lyme Regis, for sharing their ideas and knowledge; the Rev. John Affleck, of The Vicarage at Whitchurch Canonicorum, in Dorset; Hugh Jaques, Archivist to the Dorset County Council, and Mary Rose, the Assistant Archivist; Lea Salinas of the Instituto Panamericano de Geografia e Historia, in Mexico; The Bermuda News Bureau; and the staff of Mary Skiffington and Grace Rawlins at the Reference Library/Archives in Bermuda.

All ideas, interpretations and statements are, of course, entirely my own responsibility.

In conclusion, I wish to thank my family, Jill, Andre and Jason. They have patiently sought to keep themselves in the twentieth century, whilst I have usually been four hundred years away!

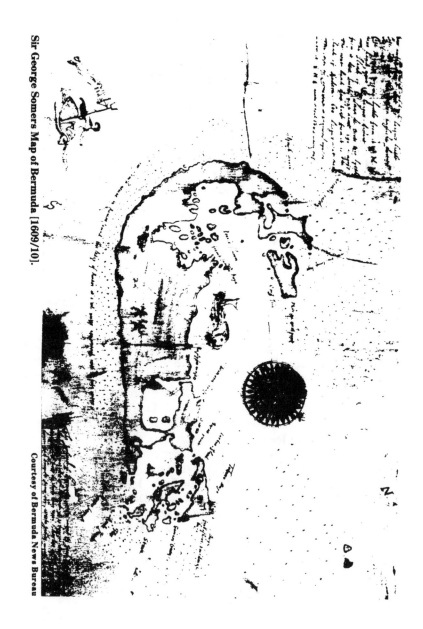

Sir George Somers Map of Bermuda [1609/10].

Courtesy of Bermuda News Bureau

1

A Background To The Somers Family

George Somers was born on Tuesday 24th. April 1554 in Lyme Regis, a town on the southern coast of England, in the County of Dorset.

He was the fourth son of John and Alice Somers. Their eldest child was Nicholas, then aged ten; next came eight-year-old John. A third son named William had been born in 1549 but he presumably died in infancy because his name does not appear in any records after his baptism.

It is not too easy to establish precisely where the surname "Somers" originates. Some authorities have suggested that it may have reached England indirectly from Mexico, having been borrowed by fifteenth century Spanish explorers from the "Suma" Indians of Central America. However, the presence of Geoffrey Sumer in the list of Essex tax-payers for 1203 would quite clearly tend to dispute that notion. Similarly, there is a Joh'ne Somer on that same County tax list for 1326. An Alice Someres crops up on the Sussex Records of 1327.

Others have suggested that the name is probably an Anglicised version of the Scottish "Simmer" or "Simmers," which was given to those folk who worked with horses. And there is yet another train of thought which links it to "Somes" or "Soames"—a name quite prevalent in East Anglia and which is a dialect variation derived from the village of Soham.

The most likely source of the family name, however, is the Old French word "Somier" for sumpter: "one who works with pack-horses or mules." In which case it could have spread throughout England at any time after the Norman Conquest of 1066. If it is indeed originally French, then it might very well have crossed over into Dorset during the fifteenth century because there is proof that another French surname—Le Hardys—reached this same county at that time. They were farmers who came from France via Jersey. By the sixteenth century, the spelling had become "Hardie" and they were firmly entrenched in and around Melbury Osmond and the town of Dorchester. (A nineteenth century descendent was author Thomas Hardy.) Maybe the Lyme Regis "Somiers" arrived with them for certainly this French origin seems to be the most likely root of the surname. Another French surname common in Dorset was Jourdain, which had roots in Limoges.

Historical records have not obliged us by carefully plotting the migrations of various members of the Somers family, although they clearly did wander quite extensively across the southern part of Medieval England. The name can be found in a host of ledgers, lists and church records throughout the outer-London counties of Surrey, Essex and Sussex; it also emerges from the shelves of dusty parchments in Suffolk, Worcestershire, Somerset and Huntingdonshire.

In government and parochial returns the name appears in different forms: Somers, Summers, Sumers, Sommers and Someres. These are obviously variations in the spelling of the same name. Even in documents which specifically refer to Sir George Somers himself, the surname is often spelt in any one of several ways; it apparently altered according to the level of education, proficiency and interest of whomever happened to be holding the quill!

As far as can be determined, George Somers' own immediate family didn't have particularily distinguished origins. They were neither rich nor poor, but members of that contented class which Napoleon Bonarparte would derisively and mockingly come to describe as "shopkeepers."

There is absolutely nothing to suggest that George's father inherited anything at all from his own parents. In fact there is no evidence to show that they even owned enough to have bothered about making a will. Nothing was ever probated.

Grandfather Somers seems to have been remarkably successful in avoiding not only the Crown scribes, but also the Church Recorders and the Town Clerk. He quite obviously existed, but his name is not to be found anywhere! We therefore tend to know far more about this elusive old man from what is **not** recorded, than from any vague fragments of information which might include him. His total absence from all land and house deeds indicates that he was hardly a man of property. The fact that he is missing from all Court and Council memoranda inevitably leads to the conclusion that he was honest and law-abiding. And his omission from tax-returns suggests that he probably did not have a regular fixed income—in which case he may have been a fisherman, or perhaps was a casual labourer on the Lyme Regis waterfront.

We may deduce that he was born in the late 1490's and married somewhere round about 1520. But all of this is conjecture for we don't even know when the wiley gentleman died.

Grandmother Somers doubtless stayed at home looking after her family. In addition to having had a son named John—George's father—there is some indication that she may have had at least two other boys: Nicholas and Robert. But again details are unreliably sketchy. Whatever became of these uncles is an untraceable mystery.

The first references to Sir George's father, John Somers, are to be found in the local militia records where, on the Official Muster Roll for 1539, he is somewhat vaguely listed as being "an able archer."

We do know that John Somers was born about 1520 and came from a relatively poor working-class background. On the other hand, it is equally as certain that through hard work he managed to raise his own family in a totally different financial environment. All suggestions that George Somers was raised amidst humble and lowly background have very little justification. He and his brothers were the sons of an ambitious merchant. John Somers has been variously described as a shopkeeper and a tradesman, but he rapidly outgrew these titles.

Life in sixteenth century England was harsh and demanding; it was a testing affair in which only the most tenacious successfully survived. These were simply not the days when the sons of paupers could freely vault into favour with the Royal Court; there was little tolerance for those who were lethargic and docile. Only achievers were rewarded in Elizabethan England—unless they happened to be blessed with regal blood-ties—and the rest were literally left to fall by the wayside.

John Somers was undoubtedly a highly-motivated, firm individual. He was also apparently a man of strict morals, driven by the determination to improve on the meagre position which he had inherited in life. He was a self-made businessman, one who rose steadily through the ranks of the Lyme Regis commercial community until he eventually became a respected Freeman of the town. He also appears to have been a good husband and father, one who encouraged and directed his sons to become individually successful in their respective careers. He imparted to each of them a set of values and standards, alongside a sense of justice and responsibility; it is ironic that young George was ultimately destined to die whilst still rigidly pursuing these same ideals and social responsibilities.

This contented, ambitious background, of course, is a noticeable contrast to the somewhat curious ideas which the early twentieth century historian F. J. Pope had of the Somers Family. If we were to believe his strange description of John Somers then we would conjure an image of a rather frail, indecisive man perpetually tottering on the brink of abject poverty; a man without sufficient money to even afford the cost of a bow-and-arrow for the Regional Muster. But all of this peculiar conjecture is far from the truth.

Certainly John Somers' name features on that oft-quoted roll of 1539, but this was nothing more than a list of men who were in the local militia. Units like these had been formed the length and breadth of England at this time and they served as a rather informal type of Reservist Army. It was a casual, somewhat spontaneous sort of thing, not particularily noted for military bearing or precision. The officers were the local landed-gentry and, for better or for worse, everyone simply fell-in behind them, at more-or-less the same time and place. Depending on how dedicated the officers were, weapons were sometimes provided; usually each man brought his own. They gathered rather infrequently, trained hardly at all and were essentially united primarily through the common prayer that they should never be called into active service. None of these loyal part-timers would have relished the thought of matching skills against fully-trained professionals from some potential invading forces.

There had been a tradition of occasional skirmishes along this part of the English coastline, mainly involving marauding pirates, looters and Frenchmen, but these invariably took the form of being brawls, short fights which never approached the proportions of full-scale military battles. Perish the thought!

But, so much for George Somers' father and paternal grandparents. What of his mother? Alas, it is very difficult to establish any information about Alice Somers. Regrettably, in keeping with the spirit of those distant days, any matters relating to the womenfolk—unless they were part of the Royal Circle—were not deemed to be particularly noteworthy. We do know that she had at least one sister called Thomasine, who may have been named after their father Thomas; but from here, the records fade into complete oblivion.

There is one final patch for the family quilt. At the same time that John Somers was being drawn into the Lyme Militia, there was also a Will or William Somers. This particular person eventually became the officially-appointed Jester to the Court of King Henry VIII. But his precise connection to the Somers family of Lyme Regis is obscur.

From all of the available evidence, we can conclude that George Somers did not come from a lowly family. In the social ladder of the mid-sixteenth century, men classified as being "merchants" stood respectfully in line just behind doctors, landowners and ministers; and they lay slightly ahead of those good folk who were described as traders, businessmen and plain, simple "gentlemen."

We also know that John and Alice Somers created a healthy and affectionate environment for their growing family. He was hardworking and well-respected; she presumably worked with equal diligence as a mother and housewife.

They did not own property but rented premises in Lyme Regis and lived above the shop. The thatched-roof building, however, has long since been destroyed. Fire always was a potential hazzard in sixteenth century Lyme.

Note: In 1993, "The Bermudian" magazine featured an interesting series of articles by John Weatherill.   In these, he sought to prove a direct connection between this Dorset Somers Family, and the Warwickshire branch of Lord Somers, Baron of Evesham. Using some credible evidence, this controversial hypothesis is based on the fundamental presumption that Sir George's brother, John Somers, inexplicably moved to the County of Warwick in 1589--which the writer admits to being hard-pressed for absolute proof. Also, if that were the case, it remains awkward to explain, beyond an amazing coincidence, John's presence in Lyme Regis on the very day that Sir George's body arrived, unannounced, in 1611; or his proven presence just 48 hours later, on 3rd.June, to claim the Will. Communications between Dorset and Warwickshire unquestionably required more travel time than available, had John still been a Warwickshire resident.

Nevertheless, "The Bermudian" articles are certainly an important reference source most worthy of further investigation.

2

**The Place And
Times Of Infancy**

In order to fully appreciate how this particular son of John and
Alice Somers could one day become an eminent Elizabethan seamen, we need to know something of his childhood. It was here
that the seeds of his character and aspirations were first sown—
planted in Lyme Regis and then nurtured by a series of events
which subsequently moulded the entire Nation.

It is impossible to have any meaningful understanding of the
surroundings in which he lived and played, without developing
some sense of feeling for Lyme itself, because the truly unique
personality of this fine and ancient port did much to create the
man who was to become perhaps to most famous of its native
sons.

Originally granted a Royal Charter in 1284, Lyme had long
cherished the right and privilege of adding "Regis" to its
name—a royal connection particularily enhanced by Edward I,
who commissioned local shipwrights to build him a galley. It was
always a proud town, a seafaring community conscious of its
heroic roots and sometimes overly-sensitive to the criticisms of
those who lived beyond the corporation boundary. It was a
fiercely independent and high spirited town.

In the sixteenth century, the layout of Lyme Regis was relatively basic. It consisted of a cluster of buildings nestled around
the mouth of the narrow River Lim, at that point where it spills

rather muddily into the English Channel. In George Somers' days, it had a population of approximately 1,200 contented souls. The houses were constructed mainly from wattle-and-daub, an interlacing of rods and twigs which was then lavishly saturated and coated with a soddy plaster. The roofs were thatched, but although the tight packing successfully managed to repel the wild winter weather, they happened to provide a fine haven for families of rats and mice—in addition to being excellent perches for the inevitable flocks of seagulls which perpetually speckled the skies.

From this cosy nucleus there radiated three principle roadways: Broad Street, Coombe Street and the old road to Charmouth. These main arteries stretched away from the town centre like spokes on a cartwheel and had the effect of slicing the area into wedge-shaped segments which pointed towards the sea. In turn, these roads were interconnected by a cobweb of paths and tracks, a network of footpaths worn through the grass and woodlands by centuries of trampling feet, cantering hooves and wobbling wheels.

As a group, the townsfolk of Lyme Regis had always held their collective head up high. There was a tradition of pride, a feeling of real worth created from a hard-earned sense of defiance and determination, and then perhaps slightly tempered by a dash of arrogance. But then each of these traits was more than justified; they were as deserved as the medals astride the breast of a wartorn veteran. For Lyme too had endured its battles.

Life in Elizabethan Lyme was not without inherent dangers; dangers produced in part by the very ground on which it deigns to stand.

Throughout its entire history, it had been commonplace for vast sections of land to suddenly cascade down into the sea. Without any apparent provocation, mighty chunks of rock and soil have frequently crashed into the churning waters below. Elsewhere, indiscriminate undercutting of the cliffline has resulted in uncontrollable avalanches of huge boulders, occurring without warning; often in the darkness of night. And subtle subterranean movements have sometimes caused unsuspecting fields to suddenly plummet inwards, as if the earth itself had gasped in shock.

The overall effect, therefore, is that the town is encircled by hills fashioned into a truly dramatic landscape, sculptured into shapes of exceptional beauty and inhabited by a group of strong-willed citizens who are quite accustomed to handling the unpredictable.

But there is yet another curse of nature which has forever tested the mettle of these hardy townsfolk: storms. Lyme lies directly along the route of the North Atlantic storm track and has always been exposed to the incessant wrath and fury of the elements. Pounding waves have consistently thrashed at the feeble breakwaters which project from the shore; sand and pebbles get hurled with angered vengeance against the houses, battering doors, windows and walls alike. Throughout centuries waves have rolled with endless fury, chiselling into the cliffs until they crumble and slither helplessly beneath the waters. During one storm in 1377, so it was told, no fewer than seventy buildings and fifty boats were swept away, swallowed by the hungry seas. In just one night, the town had been virtually wiped-out.

But with the dawning of a new day Lyme's people had always come back out; resurfacing to clear-up once more; determined to rebuild their lives. They had never thought to give in.

George Somers experienced days and nights like these from the very moment that he was born. During his childhood there must have been many times when he stood watching the work-gangs as they pulled debris from fallen chimneys and roofs; then together they braced themselves for the inevitable tragedies which lay buried beneath the rubble. It was all an inescapeable intimacy with the violence of the furious seas. It tested and challenged him as a little boy and unwittingly helped to prepare him for the final tempest which he would face as an older man.

Just like his contemporaries, George became determined, resourceful and resilient; he was a lad forged on the anvil of defiance, one to whom the act of surrendering would be instinctively foreign. He knew the sea. He watched the ugliness of her ignoble tantrums and then marvelled at the sensuous, silken beauty of her most tranquil moments.

As he gradually became older and more certain of his own physical abilities, young George Somers joined the sailors and fishermen in rescuing boats once the battering waves had begun to abate; he helped them as they blindly waded into the murky, swirling waters to grab at sunken hulls; or to haul more solemn pieces of wreckage higher up the beach, beyond harm's way. On calmer afternoons he and his friends combed the sands at low-tide, mudlarks hoping to discover treasure by poking into the beach with bits of wood. But the flotsam and jetsum rarely yielded anything of value; no Spanish gold.

* * * * * *

Life in sixteenth century Lyme Regis was remarkably hard; it made heavy demands and exacted high tolls. Its townsfolk, however, could never have been accused of weakness; they had never sought to abandon it.

From infancy, George Somers gained a personal insight into the harsh realities which lay ahead of him. Without tenderness or protective mercy it was all bluntly hammered home when he was just four years old. In 1558, his eldest brother John died. John had been a strong, healthy boy aged twelve; then one day he became sick and died. There was no complete understanding for why it had happened or whether it could have been prevented. Nobody was even too sure as to what he had died from—unless it was something he had eaten, or maybe he had caught one of those strange recurring diseases which flitted across the countryside from time to time. None of them would ever know for certain. The fact remained that John had died. It was probably God's Will.

A short service was held in the Church of St. Michael, a hundred yards up from the town centre. The Parish Church had hosted a good number of these sad gatherings since it had been first erected on that same site, in 1145. Religion played a major role in helping the people of Lyme Regis to cope with their daily hardships. John and Alice Somers, like everyone else, took their children to church each week, for that was the strict custom of the period; and they had regularily attended the special services which blessed the fishermen and sailors on their eves of departure. Then too they had certainly sat with bowed heads, as the priests lamented over the souls of those who would not be returning from their voyages. Grief was also a custom.

And so it was that John and Alice Somers took their eldest son to church for the last time, to be buried, and after the funeral they held the hands of young Nicholas and George and returned home with their private sorrow. The next year, Alice Somers gave birth to another son whom they also called John—for life must always continue. George probably hoped that he might have the chance to know this brother a little better.

* * * * * *

Beyond the cobbled streets of Lyme Regis there were other events taking place about which young George Somers could have had no meaningful understanding whatsoever. Nevertheless, these events would play a significant part in moulding not just this one small boy, but would also cast the personality and attitudes of his entire generation.

Throughout his infancy, England was experiencing deep and devastating turmoil. Other countries saw only her placid mask of green hills; the more perceptive observers may have guessed that she was casually awaiting the opportunity to snatch control of the oceans from the ageing seamen of Spain. But few suspected that in the leafy darkness of the glades and copses England was visciously disembowelling herself. Blood splattered the far side of the rolling countryside.

Without being aware of it, George Somers spent the first five years of his life under the bloody and repressive rule of Queen Mary, a spiteful Catholic zealot. He was only three months old when she married Prince Philip of Spain, son of the ailing King Charles V and heir to the Spanish throne. They were wed in Winchester, Devon, on 22nd. July 1554 by Archbishop Gardiner.

In July of the following year, Philip returned to Spain, alone. He had finally accepted the fact that Mary, for some inexplicable reason, was still not as pregnant as they had both earnestly hoped she would be. Tired and fed-up, he evidently decided that there were other things to attend to. Mary was equally as disappointed by this sad state of affairs (or lack thereof). We may never learn the exact extent of her displeasure but there is no doubt that she unleashed her frustrations on the entire country. It can be no mere coincidence that, shortly after her disgruntled husband had departed, Bloody Mary started her brief reign of terror.

And so whilst the Somers family was innocently and excitedly watching their new baby learning to crawl, elsewhere in the country hundreds of people were being put to death for "treasonable utterances." Highly sensitive to her religious convictions the Queen took any anti-Catholic sentiments to be a direct, personal attack against the Crown. In a country which was still not convinced that it really was Catholic, such utterances were not uncommon. Sadly, however, the penalty for such loose talk was death.

The wretched pages of her reign are stained with signs that Mary almost delighted in squeezing the last juices of pain from her victims. Even those wretches sentenced to be burnt for their heresies usually did so tied to a stake, with bags of gunpowder dangling around their necks as decoration. Archbishop Latimer was burnt in October 1555; the following year Archbishop Cranmer was put to death in the same spot, alongside the Archbishop of London. Literally hundreds of priests either lost their jobs, or their lives. In the vile circles of Mary's Court there were grizzly jests about "sizzling sermons," but not everyone was amused.

But resentment against Mary did not stem solely from her religious beliefs and casual brutality. It had festered since the moment when her engagement to Prince Philip had been first announced, in early 1554. This man was the very symbol of the ageless hatred and rivalry which existed between England and Spain and few expected that such animousity and mistrust could suddenly be tossed aside at the altar.

In particular, the seafaring peoples of the West Country were greatly angered by the marriage. Collectively, their sons, husbands, brothers and fathers had paid a high price in sacrifices at sea. Afterall, these were the same men who gallantly stood on the decks of Royal ships—only to be blasted into fleshy fragments by Spanish gunfire. No! The mood in this part of England was one of anger and none had stood to throw confetti upon this unsympathetic monarch whose new husband was the enemy who killed their menfolk.

In the inns and market-places of Devon, dissention seethed like a dormant volcano. Somerset was no less-disgruntled. That county was still smarting from the execution of its much-loved Earl, Edward Seymour, beheaded in 1552 on "trumped-up charges of treason" at the behest of Mary's brother King Edward. They hadn't been impressed by the last monarch and wanted little to do with this insensitive novice-Queen. And in Dorset, where George Somers was still innocently waddling his way through infancy, the atmosphere was just as ugly.

This county had been at the hub of the Queen's controversial succession and bitterness remained firmly alive. The villages and hamlets of Dorset offered little sympathy or tolerance for either Mary or her courtiers.

Apparently, as Edward VI lay on his deathbed in July 1553, he declared that Lady Jane Gray (b. 1537) should be his lawful successor to the throne and titles of the Kingdom. This charming young lass of Dorset was a descendent on the Queen's side. The Royal couple had no children of their own, probably because Edward had devoted most of his time to ransacking churches and frightening everyone with his wild, irrationable outbursts . at least, that was the sarcastic explanation offered across the tables in the inns of the county. At the time, Lady Jane was just a sweet little thing aged sixteen; the previous year she had been encouraged to marry the willowy Lord Dudley, son of the ambitious Duke of Northumberland. In short, being appointed to become the new Queen startled Jane, confused The Court—and elated her father-in-law.

A lot of bickering ensued, during which it was argued that at least Mary was the deceased's sister, and also a daughter of Henry VIII. She was flowing with regal blood, whereas Jane was merely paddling on the edges of a tributary. Just nine days after she had so unexpectedly inherited the deeds and titles to the throne, Lady Jane quite willingly relinquished it all in favour of Mary. And for her remarkable understanding, civility and public-minded cooperation, this hapless lady was duly rewarded by the new monarch on February 23rd. 1554. On that Wednesday morning, as the predawn mists began to rise over the River Thames, she and her totally bewildered husband were beheaded "for treason ".

The entire episode set the tone for the years to come.

On that particular day, many miles away from London, Alice Somers was still five months pregnant with George; but even then she must have wondered about the nature of the world into which her baby would be born.

The executions caused Dorset to erupt with more sparks and noise than an exploding keg of powder, but the uprising achieved nothing of benefit. Sir Thomas Wyat, the leader of the rebellion, was beheaded and so were two of poor Lady Jane's brothers—one of whom was Henry, the 3rd. Marquis of Dorset. Another brother was unexpectedly reprieved whilst he sat forlornly in his cell listening to the axman's handiwork on the lawn outside. Needless to say, thereafter he lived a long and tactfully quiet life.

But displeasure lingered beneath the surface, even though the hostilities had been defused, and discontent even swirled with the beer in the taverns of Lyme Regis. The townsfolk had felt especially insulted by a rumour that Queen Mary had cited one of their own Festival Days as being "heretical and baudy." It was an uncalled-for provocation which none of them needed.

Clearly, such uneasiness could not continue forever. The people of England were not prepared to tolerate the unpleasant bloodshed indefinitely. Since 1546, they had gone through the ravenous appetite of Henry VIII, the hysterical reign of Edward VI and were now emersed in the barbarity of Bloody Mary. They wanted a change.

As if in answer to a national prayer, the change came about on Wednesday 17th. November 1558. On that memorable day, the Queen died somewhat ignobly from what was delicately described as "dropsey." The only reason for mentioning that distasteful sickness here is that the unpleasant and odourous mood of the Nation appears to have collapsed at the precise moment as the Royal kidneys. The stench of Winter gloom was quickly replaced by the freshness of Spring. There was a spirit of rebirth.

The new monarch was Elizabeth I. Although she was Mary's sister, she showed no signs of having inherited the same genes. She was young, attractive and remarkably popular with her subjects. Quickly, they settled-down with excitement to watch England's most eligible bachelors strutting before her, a procession of peacocks vying for the royal damsel's hand, affections and favours. Soon people began to guess as to which of these fine suitors she would marry. They gasped at her fashionable wardrobe; they tried to copy her styles in clothing, jewelry and wigs. She towered like a beacon in the clearing fog and her subjects flocked about her, fluttering in awe and gratitude.

Elizabeth's enthronement became a signal for droves of expatriates to return home. Many of these voluntary exiles were young and dynamic; there were soldiers, adventurers and free-thinkers. They were leaders who could set a new and energetic form of government to match that of their bright, vivacious Queen. Ideas abounded and the young monarch listened. A new feeling of hope and worth was born from the ashes of those repressive years under Mary. They complimented the Court of Elizabeth I perfectly and helped to create an entirely new era.

And by one of those curious quirks of historical coincidence, the international pendulum of good fortune was also swinging in England's favour. As Spain's mighty sailors and explorers were dying, so those of England were just being born. Between 1538-1548, Spain recorded the deaths of Diego de Almagro and Hernandez Cortez; Francisco Pizarro was assassinated and his brother Gonzalo died. But at roughly this same time England could rejoice in the births of: Humphrey Gilbert, Francis Drake, Walter Raleigh, James Lancaster, John Davis, Martin Frobisher and Richard Grenville. And in Dorset, George Somers had just been born in 1554.

In every conceivable respect, the Old Order had gone. New faces stood at the helms of the ships and, like the flags which they would plant across the face of the earth, they too were English. They would lay the foundations for the global character of the next five hundred years.

George Somers, therefore, had been born at a time of dreadful domestic chaos, but as he emerged from infancy so the tides of England's future had already made a pleasing and abrupt turn. This was the Elizabethan Age of Aquarius; a time when the Nation's honour would ride to the fullest heights of international impact and influence.

George Somers' life would grow with it and when it finally came to a close, then he too would be destined to pass into the shadows. For a young boy like him, this was a remarkable time to have been born. Growing-up would be fun. Life would be exciting and challenging.

He had survived his infancy. He was now 4½ years old.

This is the forme of a Mappe sent 1527. from Siuill in Spayne by maister Robert Thorne marchaunt, to Doctor Ley Embassadour for king Henry the 8. to Charles the Emperour. And although the same in this present time may seeme rude, yet I haue set it out, because his booke coulde not well be vnderstood without the same. The imperfection of which Mappe may be excused by that tyme the knowledge of Cosmographie not then beying entred among our Marchauntes, as nowe it is.

**Robert Thorne's world map of 1527. Reproduced for
Richard Hakluyt in Divers Voyages [1582].**

3

The Carefree Youth Of A Merchant's Son

As youngsters growing-up in Lyme Regis, Nicholas, George and John Somers led vibrant and exciting lives. There was never any boredom; no lacking of things to stimulate their minds. Each day was crammed from dawn to dusk with playing, watching, listening, doing and learning.

Today, Lyme is a quiet seaside resort, small and cosy. But in the sixteenth century it was a very active, bustling port; a town handling more trade than Liverpool and rivalling Plymouth and Bristol in importance. Christopher Saxon, the Elizabethan cartographer, considered that only Southampton could match it for prominence among all of the towns along the southern coast of England.

More than anything else, Lyme was famed for three very noble traditions: trading, sailing and fishing. Each of these flavoured the town and gave a distinct colouring to the ambitions of successive generations of its youngsters.

The community is centred on the craggy rim of Lyme Bay, a minor curve in what is otherwise a heavily indented strip of shore. Protruding from the western side of the bay is a distinctive man-made feature called "The Cobb." Essentially, The Cobb is a crescent-shaped pier which stretches into the sea. Like some kindly maternal arm, it curls protectively around one side of the bay, deflecting the violent waves which would otherwise damage the coastline and splinter the boats which lie within the inner wall. Partially enclosing Lyme Bay, it is therefore The Cobb which has created a harbour for the town.

The water is far deeper along the wall of The Cobb and so it was here that trading vessels were fastened. Rowing-boats would then ferry passengers and freight over to the beach-head where they then disembarked at a wide truncated jetty known as "Cobb Gate." It was appropriately named because all merchandise had to pass through here in order to be recorded, valued, taxed and checked before finally being landed. At low-tide, horses were sometimes used to drag people and goods across the mudflats on devices similar to wooden travoise. Throughout George Somers' youth there were no buildings on the seaward side of Cobb Gate and only recently had they erected a small canon-fortification at the tip of The Cobb itself.

The chronicler Roger North likened Lyme's Cobb to a mole burrowing out to sea, adding that there was nothing like it anywhere in England except for the half-moon harbour at Scarborough, faraway to the north-east.

It was to Cobb Gate that John Somers took his three sons daily. He, of course, began each bout of business here, vying with other merchants and striving to get the best deals on the most attractive commodities. The boys eagerly stretched their necks to see what the latest ships had brought with them. Lyme Regis was not just a regional focal-point. It was a nodal centre for all merchants travelling across the sprawling countryside of England. They came not only from the Western Counties, the rural hamlets and the area's towns, but often from places as distant as London. Others even came from Wales and the remote towns in the bleaker extremities of England and Scotland.

Young George was nurtured on these exciting, hectic surroundings. He was a child weaned on the rushed ways of the transients. He heard from infancy their peculiar mixtures of accents and dialects. He stood regularly with his father at Cobb Gate, just beneath Bell Cliff at the foot of Broad Street, gawking with wonder at the curious speech of the French, Spanish and Flemish sailors who congregated there. He watched the long-frocked Arab traders furiously gesturing, lengths of silk trailing from their arms, turbans on their heads. And it must have been fascinating for him to see how easily some of his own people managed to casually switch from English into the strange sounds and mannerisms of the foreigners. It was all far from being boring.

Standing slightly aback from the noisy crowd in which his

father was haggling, he had plenty of opportunities to observe the rugged men who brought-in the captured prize-boats which they had seized somewhere further up The Channel. The boys could stand and listen to their crude banter as they discussed their dubious affairs and, from seeing them repeatedly in Lyme, they doubtless grew to recognise and know them, their shouting and arguing. Their boats were also a regular sight, the names blatantly and unashamedly Anglicised; everyone knew that the "Flower of Luce" had once been the "Fleur de Lys" when it had sailed under the flag of France, but nobody ever talked about things like that.

These swashbucklers stood out. They were men of a distinctly different breed from those who worked the domestic merchant boats up and down the coast. The differences could be noticed even through the eyes of a small boy who scarcely reached up to the level of the seamen's belt buckles. They were invariably coarser of speech and behaviour than the other sailors, and youngsters like the Somers boys realised how boisterous they were around the inns of the town. But then most of them weren't from Lyme Regis anyway and so they didn't linger for very long. As if drawn by habit and compulsion, they usually came into port, settled their affairs, did whatever it was they had to do and were gone back to sea once more.

As an impressionable boy, George Somers saw that there was an urgency to everything that they did; each moment appeared precious to them, as if it would be the last they would ever have on land. There is nothing to suggest that he ever sought to become one of these overwhelming, intimidating and uncouth renegades, although their obvious love for the sea must surely have left an indelible mark on the mind of this young boy and many of his friends.

George could at least dream of the day when he might triumphantly lead **his** crew back into Lyme Regis and tie **his** prizes to the walls of The Cobb. He could perhaps think of leading his men as they disembarked at the jetty beneath Bell Cliff and made for the sweaty interiors of the inns. That much he might well have dreamt about!

From Lyme Regis boats were continuously leaving for distant shores. Some went trading to Southern Europe, North Africa and into the Mediterranean Sea. Others, the fishing vessels, made longer journeys to the other side of the Atlantic where they engaged in trawling off the Grand Banks of Newfoundland. Ever since the duo of John and Sebastian Cabot had sailed along the coast of North Africa sixty years earlier, England had regarded the adjacent waters as her own. In fact, by 1517 over 300 fishing boats were annually plying the cod grounds—many of them coming from places like Lyme Regis. Indeed so much fishing was being carried out by the English fleets that a special Fisheries Act had been passed by Parliament in 1542, as an astute means of protecting the development and depletion of those waters.

For his part, numerous were the times when George and his brothers clambered aboard the wooden clinkered hulls of the local fishing boats and headed out in search of mackerel and pilchards. They never had to go far because the fish swam in great abundance less than a mile off the beaches. Within a couple of hours they could return to land once more, laden with enough fish not only to feed their own family, but with a surplus to sell to the customers who always lined the quayside.

In the setting sun, colourful shadows would creep along the narrow side-streets and alleyways between the buildings, just as they do today; not eerily, but protectively. And while dusk descended over the becalmed town so the smell of freshly-cooked fish would often surface above the other nightly odours of Lyme Regis. It was indeed a healthy place in which to have been born!

It might have been frustrating for an eight-year-old, but for the time-being George had to be content to listen to the sea and watch its people drifting away through the early morning mists. Where it was they went to; what they did and saw would have to remain their private secret, until he was old enough to join them and see for himself what it was that lay beyond the horizon. Meanwhile, there were lots of things to do and not all of them were connected with the watery comings and goings along the seafront.

Sometimes, George and his youngest brother John would head up Broad Street and then run the full length of Silver Street to where it slipped among the woods. There they could play for hours. It was a chance to turn their backs on the town and retreat into a world of green leaves and bushes; a place where they could act out their fantasies, play hide-and-seek and look for the nests of finches, jays or sparrow-hawks. It was a safe place, not infested by robbers; the old Saxon Road which ran roughly east-to-west about a mile north of Lyme effectively served as an informal boundary, so that anyone passing over it was virtually already in the town.

Their father doubtless told them that in his childhood the woods had been denser and far more mysterious. But the trees had gradually become so thinned-out by the demands of local shipwrights that by the 1550's they were already relying on timber fetched from places as much as eight and ten miles away.

Nicholas, George and John must have roamed through these woods for much of their childhoods. They didn't just play on their own. The wide age differences between the three Somers boys—fifteen years—meant that they were often among children with similarly mixed ages. They certainly knew John and Robert Hazzard and played with Walter Harvey and Richard Hill; their loosely-knit circle also included Richard Carpenter, the son of a leading citizen of Lyme. Then there were Richard Norris and Christopher Elmerston, two boys who became lifelong friends of George Somers. Another contemporary was Silvester Jourdain, the son of John Jourdain, and his two cousins Ignatius and John.

They were all normal fun-loving boys, although future notorieties indicate that the two leading tearaways in the group were John Hazzard and Silvester Jourdain.

As Nicholas grew older and became more interested in other things, George became responsible for young John whenever they went on these playful jaunts. When they tired of dangling, climbing and swinging from the branches, they might have charged down the grassy slopes which formed the banks of the River Lim. Then they could follow the tracks along the water's edge—gazing to watch the ducks on the embankment at Gosling Bridge, or merely looking at the steady flow of carts and horses which passed by.

Once over the bridge, they could then turn onto Coombe Street and walk back into town, crossing the old market place on George Square. It was here that passenger coaches would stopover; the occupants of these ricketty vehicles being more than eager to walk their legs back into circulation and rest their severely shaken bodies.

If the boys did not want to go into the woods and walk through the countryside, then they could always run along the beach and splash in the water; or play football on Broad Street. Actually, playing ball-games was often something of a problem for the children in Lyme. The volume of traffic up Coombe Street made the older part of the town far too dangerous and Cobb Gate was far too busy. They therefore either played on the sands or else on Broad Street.

Since 1551, Broad Street itself had presented additional obstacles for footballers. That year, the Town Council dug a water-channel the full length from top to bottom down the street and heavy fines were imposed on anyone who interferred with it in any way. The thought of having their football jostling along it must have been ominous indeed. Other than this, Broad Street was a natural steep incline which ended abruptly at the market area adjacent to Bell Cliff. Beyond that lay the sea. We can but imagine at the times that they stood and watched their ball bobbing, bouncing and rolling into the feet, vegetables, sacks, wine kegs and cackling chickens around the stalls. But then playing amidst such obstacles may have supplied an extra dash of challenge to their games; it was probably far better than playing on the flat field at the end of Silver Street where their own parents had strolled, courted and played games themselves.

When they weren't playing, they went shopping with their mother. Lyme had two markets: the one off Coombe Street, in George Square, and a smaller one ostensibly for meats at the bottom of Broad Street. There was a remarkable range of goods available to the people of sixteenth century Lyme Regis. The tariff sheets for the 1560's suggest a great amount of farm produce, lying alongside exotic fruits from the Mediterranean, rich silks and linens and wines from The Canaries, Malaga and Burgundy. There were candles, tiles from Flanders, bags of figs and copper items; bolts of coarse Honiton cloth lay near nuts, spices and offal. By the time that George Somers was shopping with his mother, trade with France had already been going on for two centuries.

Finally, there was another side to Lyme Regis—one rarely seen by outsiders; but one which was nevertheless very real and vital. There was a side to the town which totally ignored the feisty competition of trade and commerce and turned its back sharply away from the salty smell of the dockside. Like other towns throughout history, Lyme Regis liked to relax, to change the pace of daily life and enjoy pure merriment.

Particularily popular were the visits of touring theatrical groups. England was famous for its travelling players and they were as familiar to the English countryside as they were in the towns of Germany. The most prestigious groups were "The Earl of Pembroke's Players" and "The Lord Chamberlain's Men" and Lyme always felt itself to be favoured when either of these paid a visit.

On such occasions the family of John and Alice Somers received their earliest exposure to what was generally accepted as being one of the Courtly forms of entertainment. They felt honoured indeed to be seeing the same people and plays which had been presented for their Queen in one of her palaces. It was unquestionably these events which laid the foundation for

George's subsequent fascination with Shakespeare's London, as an adult.

This social highlight occurred about once per year and attracted all and sundry. From neighbouring estates came the wealthy landed gentry. They arrived on horseback or by wagon, the rich people from Uplyme and Colway Manor always bedecked in their grandest clothing; guests from London copying the high-fashions of the Queen and her Courtiers. The men wore Venetian hose fastened above the knee, with long colourful stockings stretched over their legs like leotards. On their heads they sported high-crowned hats with a jaunty feather sprouting from one side. The ladies struggled valiantly to keep abreast of the innovative ideas of their youthful Queen, and so they wore tall ruffs circled around their necks and long flowing gowns which dusted the ground, mud and puddles behind them. Although the trip from their outlying homes rarely took more than an hour, what bumpy and uncomfortable rides they must have been in the back of a wooden cart; the ladies vainly trying to keep their high impractical wigs in position as they bounced from side to side; the men gallantly trotting ahead, struggling to prevent their precariously-perched hats from being blown away!

Sometimes the visits of travelling theatres attracted monks. There was a regular passage of pilgrims going along these byways, crossing from Exeter to Marshwood and on to Sherbourne or Plymouth. Some stopped to pay homage to the relics of St. Wita at Whitchurch Canonicorum, on the other side of Charmouth, and so a detour to watch a play in Lyme Regis was not much of an inconvenience. George was therefore never surprised to see the pious monks graciously appearing in the crowded streets. They paused long enough to toss a few blessings and collect alms from their temporarily adopted flocks. After the entertainment, they again proceeded on their Holy Ways.

Unfortunately for the people of Lyme, it must have seemed all too soon that the plays were performed and the actors with their brightly decorated caravans were wending tracks to their next venue.

There were, however, a couple of other social events on the local calendar and George, Nicholas and John may have been even more excited by the days set aside for Fairs. By a Royal Decree of 1553, the 1st. of February and September 20th. were officially designated as Lyme Regis' Festival Days. There was dancing in the streets and picnics along the banks of the River Lim; the children ran, laughed and chased each other. Even the usually austere cannon at Gun Cliff was bedecked with fanciful bunting and gay flowers on these days. It was impossible for any of them to imagine what Queen Mary found "baudy and heretical."

In a port such as this, the traditional May Day was far less significant than it was further inland among the farmers, although sometimes the spirit did enter the town and a Maypole might have been erected in the grassy area just north of Silver Street. This ritual dated back to the days when farmers danced and sang in the hope of securing greater fertility for their crops and cattle. Human birth charts indicate that they may also have included their own private lives in these hopes and dreams for the year ahead! May Days had been openly condemned by the Puritans and in 1568 their leading literary propagandist, John Stubbs, had described the event as being pagan; the Maypole itself he referred to as a perverse "stynkynge idol."

The last holiday for the year was one which was completely unique to Lyme Regis. It was unobstrusively known as "Cobb Ale" and there was no other like it in the entire world. The origin of the occasion went well beyond the living memory of John Somers, but was just as valid in the 1560's as it had been during the days of his own youth. Cobb Ale was a single day set aside each year to raise funds to cover the cost of repairing The Cobb. Without regular maintenance, they all knew that the wave-battered Cobb would collapse, and with it would go their collective futures. Thus, Cobb Ale was really a fund-raising dinner organised by The Guild and served to invited merchants and landowners; in exchange for the feast, each was expected to make a contribution to this worthy cause.

By all contemporary accounts, Cobb Ale was consistently a resounding success. John Somers, as a member of The Guild was always there to help with arrangements and his sons looked forward to the day when they too could become participants. Evidently some of the contributors became intoxicated, presumably with the joy of giving, and it was not unknown for the day itself to actually extend into a week or so. However, Cobb Ale assured the survival of The Cobb for another year and thus guaranteed the continuance of Lyme Regis. (Sadly enough, it was banned permanently in 1610—branded as being too debauching.)

* * * * * *

George Somers and his brothers went through their childhoods experiencing laughter and happiness; they played in the woods, went shopping with their mother and followed their father as he wandered along the waterfront, haggling within the world of commerce. They were always kept occupied, interested and entertained.

However, above these distractions, the sea remained the most dominating feature for George. He saw it everyday; could probably see it from his bedroom. He and his brothers could smell it above all other daily smells. It overpowered and permeated everything which he did and thought. By the time that he was twelve years old, it had become obvious that the signposts of his youth were already pointing him in this one direction.

The map of the Americas by Filips Galle. Prefixed to
Hakluyt's translation of Pietro Martiro d'Anghiera, Decades [1587].

4

Growing Towards The Sea

In 1567, George Somers became a teenager. It was a moment which passed without recognition, no fanfare; was perhaps quite irrelevant. The significance is really retrospective, of interest because by this stage of his life his future had become substantially settled. His choices of a career had not been whittled-down through coersion or pressure; no-one forced him to go to sea. In some respects, however, this particular son of John and Alice Somers was guided towards the sea by a conspiracy of circumstances. Fortunately it suited his interests and he excitedly watched everything converge with eyes wide open.

In order to appreciate this we need to understand that George Somers was the product of a different period of history; we must remember too that he had been raised in the glaring seafaring traditions of Lyme Regis and, furthermore, was the second eldest son of an ambitious Elizabethan merchant.

The dynamic momentum which swept England with the succession of Elizabeth I percolated enthusiasm and faith directly into individual homes. Everyone wanted to be a part of this new spirit; people lost former inhibitions and confidently struck outwards at ever-widening circles of opportunity. Like others, John Somers was drawn into the frenzy and within his own household there evolved a sequence of succession; he adopted all of the characteristics of a family business based upon rights and responsibilities. It was a pattern typical of all Elizabethan merchants. As their business interests grew, so whole areas blocked themselves off to await the interests, abilities and aptitudes of another member of the family. In turn, each son's potential would be cultivated and harnessed to the business. Nicholas, George and John would each have their parts to play when they became old enough and John Somers himself would steadily climb from being a shopkeeper, to a trader, and on to becoming a respected merchant and Freeman of Lyme Regis.

As the eldest surviving son, Nicholas was the first to become an active partner with their father. He was, of course, much older than his two brothers and by the time that George had reached thirteen, Nicholas was already a grown man of twenty-three. He was now well-versed in the general daily duties of their affairs and tended to take full responsibility for these, freeing his father to spend more time purchasing goods at the dock. He was also familiar with the patterns of trade which they conducted with such outlying villages as Charmouth, Seaton, Beer, Wootton and Stantongabriell. And he had gone with his father to the larger settlements of Honiton, Plymouth and Dorchester.

By 1570, Nicholas Somers had firmly carved his own niche in the commercial life of Lyme Regis and this enabled John Somers to pay more attention to the aptitudes and interests of his second son. He now became sensitive to George's hopes and skills and so turned to help guide this next son's future.

George naturally received an informal education which was unavoidably biased towards commerce. He sat quietly listening to his father and Nicholas as they chatted during supper about sales and costs; through them he developed a feeling for the volume and diverse nature of their business activities, as well as trading within the region as a whole. In the dim, flickering candlelight he first heard his parents discussing payments for various taxes and levies.

The Ship Levy was one of these which he heard them talk about. It was a charge made against everyone in England, so that they would all contribute to the cost of maintaining the country's naval defences. (In 1578, John Somers would be assessed to pay the princely sum of two shillings-and-sixpence.) Around the house he also became familiar with the irregular payment of "Ransom Money." It had become a normal procedure for captured seamen to be released upon payment of a ransom; such monies were usually collected through public contributions organised by the clergy of the parish in which the prisoner lived. Everyone in Lyme Regis had made this sort of donation many times for their own unfortunates; and at the time that George was actually being born, his parents had contributed towards a national collection which was then underway to secure the release of none other than Sir Martin Frobisher. (He had been languishing in a Portuguese prison in Africa for a full year before a mutually acceptable ransom figure could be agreed upon.)

By simply being with his father and brother as they bargained, bartered and dealt with other traders, George was constantly learning new things related to business. He walked with them when they cleared goods with the Customs officials and learnt about the complex procedures which that involved. By merely being with Nicholas and their father, he began to recognise various buyers and sellers and could anticipate which commodities each might be unloading from a particular boat. He learnt the names of the ships and got to know where each was from and where it travelled to.

In this casual, indirect manner, all sorts of things were learnt. We may but wonder at the number of times that he had sat on Buddle Bridge, a few yards up from where his mentors were busily haggling; sitting there atop the walls of this small thirteenth century bridge, with the gentle trickle of the River Lim flowing underneath, it would have been impossible to have escaped hearing the stories and yarns of the sailors and merchantmen who lurched nearby. Perhaps whilst flicking tiny stones into the water below, or when merely tapping his heels against the decorative stonework, he also listened to reports of the latest expeditions of Sir John Hawkins—or overheard word of an attack recently launched by Frobisher against the Spaniards. From here he certainly heard the names of the remote countries, islands and ports which he hoped to visit for himself some day.

It was also whilst ambling around Cobb Gate with his father and brothers that George Somers might have first casually noticed Mr. and Mrs. Philip Heywood out for a stroll with their four-year-old daughter, Joane. The little girl was then learning to walk and keep her balance and probably warranted only passing attention from George and his teenage friends. How could any of them know, at that moment, that less than two decades later this tiny tot would become his wife?

But George Somers was not permanently anchored to the waterfront of Lyme Regis. Part of growing-up also gave him the chance to make trips inland when Nicholas or his father visited customers and made deliveries. Then, he gained another perspective on the villages and towns of the Dorset hinterland.

Thanks to the diligence of such travellers as Celia Fiennes, we have a detailed picture of the landscape, roadways and scenery which they saw. We know that they travelled along exceedingly narrow lanes, each so overgrown and congested with mud and landslips that it was impossible for any more than just one horse to pass; at times embankments had washed down, blocking the way and causing thickets and trees to skid onto the paths "swallowing them up." But the countryside was attractive, providing that they could afford to take their eyes from "the weyes" and enjoy it. Beyond Lyme's own ring of hills, the country was a mixture of rich pastures for sheep and cows and elsewhere it gave way to extensive orchards where apples grew in great abundance. Neighbouring Somerset was well-known for its cider.

Many of the lanes were pebbled with large smooth stones, making it awkward for the horses of foreigners to walk comfortably. But local travellers were accustomed to these surfaces and had little problem in guiding their animals beyond the bushes, thickets and slender paths which everyone used to get from village to village. Some of the routes were so narrow that carts could not be used on them, in which case the people carried their merchandise on the backs of their horses, fastened to wooden frames which dangled either side of the animals' bellies.

A visit to Honiton must have been quite enjoyable because the roads were covered with fine gravels between there and Axminster. The latter was just a little market town, but Honiton itself was a large place where they made fine bonelace "in imitation of Flanders and Antwerp"; it had a large church with a round tower and a spire, and there was an active weekly market to which traders from all over the district flocked to buy and sell.

These excursions were eventful and challenging; a commercial necessity which afforded George Somers the opportunity to explore and see new places. The lanes may have been stony and dirty and "pretty much up and down like the other parts of these counties" but it all helped to broaden his experiences and made him a little more worldly. The land was so ricketty and bumpy on the other side of the crest of Lyme's hills that more than one wag went on record as saying that the mere thought of having to travel inland had caused many of the town's menfolk to rush off to sea!

George Somers, however, had always felt instinctively drawn towards the sea and whenever opportunities arose he would board one of the smaller trading boats and join the crew for a short trip along the coast to towns like Sidmouth, Exmouth and Budleigh Salterton. Once he was in the midst of the sailors he became entranced by their conversations. He listened to them talking about the increasing popularity of galleons, boats which had the character and appearance of the old-fashioned rowing galleys, but which were pure enchanting sail. He must also have heard them chatting about "Triumph," a boat launched in 1561 which was destined to remain the biggest vessel afloat right up to the end of the century. "Triumph" was then the true wonder and amazement of England and there was always space in a crowded cabin for any sailor who could claim to have seen her, or sailed on her. It was said that she was 100 feet long and 40 feet wide.

They discussed technical matters too, and George sat eagerly trying to benefit from their knowledge. They spoke of the revolutionary new tiller which was then being introduced—a system whereby a vertical level called a 'whipstaff' passed through a pivot to the upper deck. The shipbuilders of Lyme Regis had also discussed this innovation in trying to incorporate it into their own inimitable designs. And there was always much talk about guns and firepower; the use of a spinning hand-canon called an arquebus, which many warships were just beginning to carry on special mounts fastened to the stern castle. Others spoke from experience about the range and size of weapons which could be conveniently packed between the recently-developed twin deckings.

George's role in the family business had by now become clear. With his interest in the sea and ships, plus a sincere yearning to sail on boats far larger than the local paquettes, it had become logical that he should become a merchant-adventurer. It would be his responsibility to cultivate relationships with traders further along the coast and to establish commercial links with more distant ports. He would have to undertake to expand the family enterprise into new commodities and hitherto untouched markets. It would be incumbent upon him to venture well beyond the reaches of those places already tapped by their competitors in Lyme.

In 1569, when these prospects had begun to solidify, John Somers must have been a proud and contented man indeed. Certainly none of them had tried to force young George to go off to sea, but it was plainly beneficial to their mutual interests if he did. John Somers' blueprint for the family's success was firmly in place and the future looked bright.

None of this was idealistic day-dreaming and it would be a grave disservice to the name of John Somers if it were inferred that his ambitions were the afterbirth of fantasy. On the contrary, many Elizabethan families charted their futures in this same way—although not all of them had the same determination and perseverance as the people of Lyme Regis, to see it through to fruition. All over the West Country, others were doing the same as John Somers and they each had the faith that their hopes would come true—albeit with a combination of willingness, luck and a generous dose of prayer.

As a youth, George knew that he could hardly expect to leap into command of the nearest boat; nor could he assume that his father's business contacts would enable him to acquire either rank or respect. He was quite old enough to appreciate that the climb would be arduous, that the yardarm was slippery.

And he was old enough too, to accept the realities which such a life would offer. He could have harboured no illusions about the nature of a sailor's life once it had been stripped of its romance and glory. Irrespective of whether he planned to cautiously trade along the shores of Europe and Africa, or whether he hoped to cross the vastness of the great oceans, George Somers knew perfectly well what lay in store.

On endless occasions, he had stood with his friends on the waterfront of Lyme Regis, joining them as they apprehensively waved farewell to their fathers and brothers. With them he had endured the weeks, months and sometimes years which would come and go before they ever returned. Lyme was accustomed to having its menfolk away like this; families were well aware of the need to show patience whilst they awaited the return of their loved ones. They were all quite familiar with the sensations which gnawed at their insides; feelings not born from impatience but rather the result of that endless anguish of knowing and hearing nothing. There was never any real way to deal with the silence and lack of reliable information. There was never an instant way for them to find-out whether their men were still at sea because they were chasing fabulous fortunes . . . or whether they had long-since perished, soon after losing sight of land. Only time would let them know whether their husbands had been slaughtered on an uncharted stretch of coast, or whether they were still alive out there, anxiously struggling to survive another season after being shipwrecked on some uninhabited island.

The sea offered no guarantees and the family of John and Alice Somers knew this. They had grown to be sympathetic and sensitive to the feelings of their seafaring neighbours; they shared with all of Lyme Regis in the agonies of uncertainty—and George Somers himself knew perfectly well what it was like to be among those who the sailors left behind.

He had no illusions. But he now knew what he wanted to do.

5

Contemporaries And Heroes

George Somers was sixteen when, in 1570, his father was made a Freeman of Lyme Regis. This was an honour to which all merchants aspired and it established John Somers quite firmly as a member of the commercial community of south-western England. It was a title which brought local responsibilities and demanded a regular input of ideas and opinions towards the development of the town. But it rewarded the title-holder with exceptionally beneficial trading opportunities which were otherwise not available to the other merchants. From such a cherished position the family of John Somers acquired personal social standing and financial benefits.

During his late teens and early twenties, George Somers continued to broaden his experiences as the seafaring son of a merchant. At home and around the town he became evermore knowledgeable about trading practices and the commodities market as a whole; he continued to make inland excursions with his father and brother and developed an ever-widening awareness of the needs and potentials of each village and hamlet. Then, of course, whenever the chance arose he enthusiastically clambered onto the decks of coastal traders and worked his way as one of the crew. With each successive trip his competence grew and his responsibilities consequently increased. He learnt about tides and currents, winds, stars; he watched how the captains managed their men in order to make them more effective. He checked the off-loading and unloading of the merchandise which they carried.

Unless some hitherto unknown private letters are unearthed, it is improbable that we shall ever know for certain just when it was that he made his first major voyage, or even where he went to. It is more than reasonable to speculate that it was probably between 1568 and 1574, when his latent talents and burning ambitions were maturing. We might also guess that he most likely sailed with one of the regular small trading fleets which made their way along the coast of France, across the Bay of Biscay and then headed into the Mediterranean Sea, or turned out towards The Canary Islands. Unfortunately there is no proof for such notions.

Surprisingly enough, the expeditions which were made during the Elizabethan period are remarkably well-documented. However, although we are free to roam among the meticulous records of Richard Hakluyt and other dedicated chroniclers, the name of George Somers is nowhere to be found in the twenty years after 1564—when we know for sure that he was making his earliest sea ventures. There are details and descriptions of literally hundreds and hundreds of ships; we know where they went, what they did and who was on board. We can readily locate the facts of Stephen Burrough's adventures "among the Samoeds," Thomas Alcok's trip to Persia and the dashing escapades of David Filie in the western Mediterranean. We may trace the exploits of John Foxe in North Africa or follow the West Indies expeditions of Bristol merchants Andrew Barker and John Oxnam. We can examine the trading permits granted for Englishmen to deal in places as far apart as the valley of the River Ob, through to the towns of The Levant. But nowhere is there reference to anyone named Somers.

This, on the other hand, should not be taken to mean that he simply was not at sea during this period for George Somers was never a true landlubber. Most references are based upon official reports or interviews with those who participated in the voyages. It is true that many of these accounts refer intimately to the names of musketmen who performed with special valour, or include mention of individual crewman who rowed ashore on some obscure headland; however, these same accounts were not intended to provide full lists of everyone aboard each ship. More to the point, we should note that those contemporary papers are littered with vague mention of "a merchant" or "a gentleman"— any one of them might have been George Somers of Lyme Regis. Similarly there is no way of knowing whether he was among the un-named middle or lower ratings who were often neglected when it came to lists. Just as easily he could have been one of those shadowy persons merely identified as "a gentleman adventurer."

With absolute certainty, however, we do know that he became one of the most respected navigators of the era and that by the time he was thirty he had been given full command of his own ship. Quite obviously he must have developed his skills by travelling on boats which went to the likes of Plymouth, Teignmouth and Dartmouth, before then beginning to travel further afield to the ports of Europe and its off-shore islands.

During the course of the 1570's, the family of John Somers began to move in more influential circles. In doing so, the scope of opportunities for George and his brothers correspondingly became wider.

It was somewhere about 1573 that John Somers found himself to be on the most cordial terms with John Williams. He was the owner of Colway Manor, a grand estate on the outer rim of the Lyme Regis boundary-line. With his son Henry and daughter-in-law Isabella, he had purchased the property from Sir George Carew in 1544. The holdings of the Williams family by now extended all over Dorset, to Tyneham and the quaintly-named hamlet of Winterbourne Herringstone. Both of his sons, Henry and Bruen, owned more land elsewhere in the region.

But it is the relationship of the two fathers which is of importance here, for their association had significant repercussions for George Somers and provided the foundations for a friendship which would subsequently help to guide his entire life.

A succession of distinguished historians confirms that among those who frequently visited Colway Manor were Walter and Catherine Raleigh. They were a wealthy, middle-aged couple who had a teenaged son named Walter, after his father. It was both natural and inevitable that these two neighbouring landbarons should socialise, meeting from time-to-time to share company, conversation and a glass of port in the delightful foothills of The Moors. Raleigh's own property covered vast reaches of shrub and farmland dispersed all the way from Plymouth to Salterton Budleigh, barely twenty miles from Lyme Regis. His estates also embraced those of his wife. Catherine Raleigh had been born on the rambling holdings of Sir Philip Champeroun, her father, at Modbury in Devon. Through her marriage to the late Sir Otho Gilbert, she had subsequently added some of his land around Compton and Dartmouth—as well as their two sons: Adrian and Humphrey Gilbert.

John Somers and John Williams were unquestionably known to each other. They were, afterall, members of the same small business community and lived not much more than a mile apart. It was through him that John Somers met the senior Walter Raleigh and his charming wife; quite probably whilst their parents chatted inside Colway Manor, sons Walter and George played, became acquainted and talked outside, somewhere in the gardens. The familiarity which developed between the Somers, Raleigh and Williams families provided a major link in the chain of events which fashioned the life of George Somers. It provided him with a direct channel into one of the foremost merchant-trading families in the country and gave him direct access to Walter Raleigh's own brothers, Adrian and Humphrey Gilbert. These were two of the leading seamen in the whole south-west, mariners who had travelled widely and explored afar. They were also at the forefront of the small group of sailors who were then working hard to evolve effective ideas about colonisation—a premise which proposed the permanent occupation of 'unclaimed lands' by English families. These two brothers had a marked impact on both Walter Raleigh and George Somers and helped to feed their future dreams for creating Virginia.

Certainly through Colway Manor and its distinguished guests, John Somers discovered that he had opened the way for his son to enter the periphery of the all-important ring of seamen who lived-in or sailed from Plymouth. It gave him the chance to be acquainted with Richard Hawkins, the son of the legendary Sir John Hawkins who, that year, was working in London as Controller of the Navy. The mutual love for the sea became a bond between them.

George Somers was far from being unusual in having this great desire to go to sea. Throughout the West Country other parents similarly hoped that their sons would become sailors; many did.

In 1550, John Davis had been born near Dartmouth, in Devon. By the time that he was sixteen he was already sailing under the Gilbert brothers and many must have been the times when he noticed his captain's half-brother standing on the quayside, watching them sail away. In his lifetime, Davis would become Elizabeth's leading Arctic explorer—his name immortalised in The Davis Strait, in Northern Canada.

Another contemporary was Francis, the son of the Reverend and Mrs. Robert Drake. Francis Drake enjoyed none of the inherited privileges of Walter Raleigh; neither did he have the advantages available to the son of a Freeman from Lyme Regis. The Drake family was fairly poor—so much so that because he was older than his brother Thomas, Francis was sent out to work when he was still just a little boy. The prime personal benefit from this predicament was that he was apprenticed to a neighbour who owned a trading barke. Therefore Francis Drake spent his childhood crossing the English Channel to France and Zeeland; when his bachelor boss died, he was bequeathed the boat.

Richard Grenville was another young man eager to prowl the seas. He was born in Cornwall in 1542 and was a cousin to Walter Raleigh. He soon joined the fleets of Hawkins and Humphrey Gilbert and had become a recognised seaman by his mid-teens. In Somerset, Ferdinando Gorges had been born in 1560; although younger than either Raleigh or George Somers, he was no less enthusiastic about his career—and he eventually shared their fascination with colonisation by helping to found the state of Maine, in North America.

In 1552, the same year of Raleigh's birth, Richard Hakluyt and William Cavendish were born in distant London. Both would become instrumental in establishing the colony of Virginia.

The remarkable thing about the lives of each of these men is that by the end of the century they would have encountered one another—and each found his path crossing with that of George Somers.

All of the younger members of this extraordinary circle of mariners had their role models; seamen to whom they could turn for inspiration and perhaps try to emulate. But two sailors in particular tended to dominate the chatter along the docks and in the market places, their exploits carried on the lips of strolling minstrels. For this new generation of sailors, their heroes were Sir John Hawkins and Sir Martin Frobisher, men whose names had long been household words. Their changing fortunes had become the barometers of England's wealth; their exploits helped to dictate the very mood of the Nation.

Fishermen who ventured no further than up and down their own bits of coastline did so confident with the knowledge that somewhere out there in the English Channel drifted the mighty galleon of Martin Frobisher. He patrolled the area continuously between 1556 and 1565. Born in Yorkshire in 1539, he roamed those waters for all of George Somers own childhood; he had been captured by Barbary pirates and had fought renegades all the way from Africa across into the Caribbean. He was the protector of English merchantmen and had been granted a permit by the Queen which enabled him to attack and capture foreign treasure ships. He was bold and wealthy and the public had been shocked when, on one occasion, his zealous pursuit of a Spanish frigate had caused one of the jealous Royal Advisors to accuse him of being a pirate!

The second heroic figure was Sir John Hawkins, the latest sailor in a long line from this prosperous seafaring family. Born in Plymouth in 1532, he was the son of Wiliam Hawkins the town's mayor and its richest citizen. Like no others before them, this family dangled the prospects of wealth before a struggling Nation and fellow mariners saw this family as the promise of what they too could achieve. They were the symbol of glory, fame and fortune. Sir John himself had become a prominent figure for having had the nerve to encroach upon the long-active Spanish slave-trade between Africa and the West Indies. Spain saw him as a sly, impertinent interloper in this lucrative business; England saw him as a hero, brazen and brave.

There was never any need for either Frobisher or Hawkins to advertise for crew. Men waited in long queues for the mere honour of being able to say that they had served under them. George Somers does not seem to have sought to join either of these legends because his interests remained purely those of a merchant-sailor; he was more interested in commerce than he was in the pugnacious encounters of privateering. However, it was an option which he knew to be there should he seek to take advantage of it later. And he showed no interest in following Raleigh to The Lowlands, to which Walter went with one of his Champeroun relatives in order to gain some practical battle experience. His energies remained firmly directed towards matters which might enhance his life as a merchant-sailor.

But even though Frobisher's galleons tried to protect them, many men continued to die before the blast of Spanish cannon; others of them benefitted from the explorations of John Hawkins and the Gilbert brothers, but it was a fact of life that men from Lyme often never returned from their voyages.

George Somers and Walter Raleigh were equally as alike as they were dis-similar. Both had grown into being hardworking, dedicated men: they took their careers seriously. Each had pleasing dispositions and manners, were well-liked. And they were both handsomely endowed with all of the vital, nebulous, ill-defined qualities which made good natural leaders. The main differences lay on the fact that Walter Raleigh had been born into the rich Upper Class of English society, a position which made it incumbent upon him to assume the duties of being a public servant and one of the country's leaders. George Somers had none of these pressures or responsibilities. He didn't have to train to be a soldier—although this certainly made him no less brave and courageous.

By the age of twenty-five, George Somers had garnered extensive commercial and sailing experience. He had already acquired a local reputation for being a successful sailor and was now poised on the brink of making a name for himself which would take his popularity far beyond the confines of Lyme and Dorset. It was 1580. Within a decade he would become a hero to others.

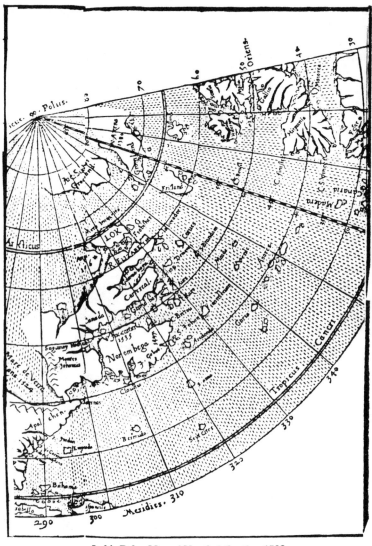

Lok's Polar Map of North Atlantic—1582.

6

The Domestic Life

In 1582 George Somers married Joane Heywood. He was twenty-eight and she was a young lady aged only nineteen.

They were both from Lyme and had unavoidably known one another for most of their lives, although there is nothing to indicate that this had been a childhood romance. There is nothing about his personality or behaviour to suggest that he had anything more than casual flirtations before he got married; nothing to show that he was a womaniser. Unlike Walter Raleigh and Robert Devereaux, the Earl of Essex, he does not appear to have cultivated much fascination for what was delicately referred to as 'the pastime of wenching.'

This, however, does not necessarily imply that he was quiet or withdrawn. Elizabethan seamen were notorious for being highly visible when they were ashore, parading in their finery with the proud gait of peacocks. George Somers certainly strutted with the best, and just as effectively. Joane Heywood, without doubt, married a most handsome and eligible bachelor and was surely the envy of other young ladies who were seeking such a grand prize as him.

Joane Heywood was born on 17th. December 1563, when her future husband was already nine years old. Actually, she was the second daughter with that name born to Philip Heywood and his wife. An earlier child had been born on 29th. February 1560, but she died soon after birth. (In various documents, her name is also spelt Joan or Jane Hayward.)

Her father is described as being a "Yeoman," a title which

placed him a few steps beneath the full-blooded landed-gentry of sixteenth century England. He was a minor landowner, a middle-class farmer who, by definition, owned sufficient property to have paid an annual land-tax for 40 shillings—no small sum in those distant days! As a Yeoman he was entitled to serve on local juries and he was also afforded the right and privilege of being able to cast a vote in various district elections. He was well-known in Lyme Regis especially among the agricultural community and his was a familiar face to the merchantmen of the town. Both fathers were therefore well-acquainted with one another and shared in the civic respect granted to those who stood close to the threshold of becoming "gentlemen."

John Somers and Philip Heywood had several things in common—social standing, financial security and ambition—and the wedding of their respective son and daughter could have met with nothing but mutual approval and consent. Precisely why George Somers decided to marry at this exact moment is, however, another issue; the couple certainly didn't have to. His reasons were probably no more complex than that fact that it was opportune, convenient; merely time that he was married.

Both of his brothers were already married and by the time that George joined them among the ranks of the wedded, they had both become fathers with infant sons. His eldest brother, Nicholas, had become an established man of independent means by 1578—at which point his name features on lists for taxes and levies. He married in that year and by August of 1580 his wife gave birth to a boy who they named Nicholas. Nicholas' progress as a merchant had apparently been marked by success. Nothing is known about his wife.

George's younger brother John was also a husband and father. He had likewise married sometime about 1578 and, by March of the following year, his wife had borne a baby boy called John. As the first Somers grandchild, the infant was named after his grandfather; it was the ultimate sign of respect. John and his wife had a second child in June 1582, just a few months after George and Joane had exchanged marriage vows. This baby, a daughter named Amy, died shortly afterwards, however.

The wedding of George Somers and Joane Heywood was a grand affair which merged two fairly prominent Lyme Regis families and symbolised the uniting of their parents' aspirations. For George Somers there was a fringe benefit. As part of her dowry, Joane brought into the marriage three houses in Lyme—property which would not only give the couple a small instant source of extra income, but would also act as vital collateral for any of their own future projects.

It was an ideal marriage, in many respects. There were distinct similarities about their backgrounds and upbringings, with the bonus of Joane's familiarity with agriculture and country-life providing the perfect balance for her husband's involvement with seafaring. Each therefore had an area of experience and knowledge about which the other knew very little; each would be able to provide valuable input into different facets of their marriage. They complimented each other almost perfectly. Clearly, she had to accept the distinct drawbacks and worries of being the wife of a merchant-seaman; there would be months of uncertainty when he was at sea, periods of great loneliness. But she appreciated all of these things before he had proposed to her and she accepted them in stride. Their major disappointment was that they never had any children.

Within the first five years of married life, George and Joane Somers had increased their private wealth to such an extent that they were able to make a substantial investment in property near Whitchurch Canonicorum—a tiny hamlet on the other side of Charmouth, on the road to Dorchester. In 1587 they bought the freehold lease to 106 acres of farmland on the outskirts of Whitchurch and the life-lease on the 200 acre estate of nearby Berne Manor. They had no problem in continuing to rent most of the land to other farmers and quickly settled-down to the excitement of furnishing and decorating the main house in which they would eventually live. As a result of George Somers' business activities they continued to live in Lyme Regis and didn't officially change their permanent resident out to Berne, until later.

Whilst perhaps lacking the superficial grandeur of many of the other West Country's larger manors, such as Colway, Sherbourne or Buckland, Berne Manor was nevertheless delightfully situated. It had been built amidst the rolling countryside of Dorset and sat perched on a slight rise from which, on a clear day, the distant sea might be discerned. There were trees on the overlooking hillsides and open green fields all around. It was nestled in an area interlaced by the same narrow, twisting lanes which he had so frequently travelled in his earlier days. Bushes of brambles, honeysuckle and blackberries covered their banks. Sheep and cows ambled across the fields nibbling at the rich, healthy grass which flourished everywhere throughout the County.

This was an area of highly desireable farmland and Dorchester, only 18 miles away, was the centre of some of the best pastureland in the entire region. It was said that within a radius of 3 miles from that town there were thousands and thousands of oxen and sheep. One contemporary traveller remarked that the area was also "very fruitful for orchards, plenty of apples and pears ..."

By purchasing Berne Manor, George Somers had joined the ranks of two other prominent Elizabethan who owned property in the area. Sir Francis Drake owned the sprawling Buckland Estate, just five or so miles southwards of Dorchester; and Walter Raleigh had come into the rights of Sherbourne Manor, to the north-west of Lyme Regis. He was already familiar with the Williams' family of Colway Manor and through Raleigh he got to know the eminent owner of Wilton Hall, on the London side of Salisbury—Sir Henry Herbert, Earl of Pembroke, and his family. George and Joane Somers had therefore become members of the landed-gentry of the West Country and through such contacts enriching avenues would now begin to open, right into the highest and most influential circles of English society.

They were, of course, already well-known to the leading families around Whitchurch Canonicorum. The Coxens, Colliers and Husseys all owned property in the community. Other dignitiaries had their homes in the neighbouring countryside, such as Sir John Jeffrey of Catherstone and John Wadham. Wadham had been born in Catherstone but had spent most of his life in Weymouth. He devoted his working years, however, to serving as the official Recorder of Lyme Regis—a position which had made him a longstanding associate of George Somers. (He died shortly after the Somers settled permanently at Berne and was buried in the churchyard at Whitchurch in 1584.) Other neighbours in Whitchurch Canonicorum were John and Friediswide Every, a pleasant family who worked several acres closeby with their son, John Junior.

Whilst Berne Manor may have lacked the stately appearance of other large estates, it was impressive nevertheless. The main entrance to the house opened onto a long hallway, in which there were thoughtfully placed stools and side-tables upon which guests could rest their hats, gloves and cloaks. Off to one side there was a small cupboard in which the domestic staff kept their aprons, gardening boots and items for daily housework. Down at the far end of this hallway was the door leading into the kitchen.

The kitchen at Berne was designed so that it could serve not just the residents themselves, but was also kept in a state of readiness in the event of unexpected guests. Travel in the late Middle Ages was an eventful and demanding undertaking; a challenge with a great deal of the unexpected about it. Broken

wheels, tired horses and weary passengers were always anticipated of any journey. Wealthier travellers consequently tended
to follow roads which enabled them to pause, and even sleep
overnight in the more comfortable surroundings of a friend's
home, en route. Berne, therefore, was organised to accomodate
such sudden arrivals and the kitchen boasted facilities which
included a great fire with five spits, large baking trays, a
cauldron, enormous serving platters, an impressive array of
silver and pewter pots, pans and mugs.

Off the main central hallway was another door, leading into
the main parlour—a room which occupied virtually half of the
entire downstairs area of the house. In here George and Joane
Somers would entertain their friends, families and visitors. On
quieter nights, in front of the blazing open-hearth fire, she would
embroider whilst George sat at the large table in the far end of
the room pawing over his maps, charts and accounts books.

The master bedroom was directly above this room; the
chimney-breast in fact continued upwards from the parlour and
was incorporated into the wall and fireplace of their bedroom.
Upstairs there were eight different bedrooms of varying sizes
and shapes, each intended to sleep guests and servants with
some degree of comfort. Each had a bed, blankets, feather
mattress and pillows. There were cupboards and chests in most
of them, curtains at the windows and rugs on the floor.

One of the smaller bedrooms adjacent to the master bedroom
was used by George's personal manservant. At various times,
this position had been held by George Bird and Robert Waters.
In here, were kept The Master's dress jackets, footwear and
other items of "public" apparel. Joane Somers' maid slept in a
slightly smaller room with only a cupboard and chest in which to
store her own few personal effects. The Mistress of the house
was always dressed and prepared in the privacy of her own
sleeping quarters and so Joane's gowns were always kept in the
closet in the corner of her own bedroom.

At the rear of the house, above the kitchen, was another
chamber set-aside as servant's quarters. It always had two beds
in it and was thus probably the one used by a married couple who
shared in the duties of cooking and cleaning. They may also have
assumed general responsibilities for overseeing other staff and
gardeners, for in one corner of their room was kept a selection of
half-a-dozen pikes. Civil conflict had grown in recent years, with
the rising impact of the Puritans, and localised rebellions had
become a constant potential danger. Against the background of a
tradition which had made the people of the West Country always

on the alert for attacks from marauding Frenchmen and renegades, there had evolved the habit of being forever ready to
defend house, property and loved ones. From this bedroom,
therefore, the staff could get their weapons and thwart an
assault on the Manor!

There was always a great deal to do at Berne and gradually
George and Joane amassed a tasteful array of carpets, curtains
and furniture to decorate their home. In due course there would
be taffetas and silks; carpets from India and Turkey; covers from
Arras with golden threads. But such things took time and his
increasingly more frequent trips down to The Canaries, Azores
and Mediterranean had not yet reaped such adequate prizes.

Where precisely George Somers was getting enough money to
fund such an affluent life-style, of course, is a moot point.
Unquestionably the fortunes of the Somers family as a whole had
given them prosperity during the decade before and after
George's marriage to Joane Heywood. Having become a Freeman Lyme in 1570, John Somers had wasted no time in using all
of his privileges as a passport to potential wealth. As the Somers'
mercantile activities expanded, so did the workloads of each
member, and so did the financial rewards which came to
Nicholas, John, George and their father.

There has always been suspicion that George Somers private
fortune owed far more to the mis-fortunes of others, than it did
to his own business acumen; that the losses of ships and cargoes
from less-friendly countries were put to his personal benefit. It is
indisputable that his ultimate wealth owed much to later expeditions which he made around the North Atlantic, and from battles
which he fought during the 1590's. It was conventional to plunder
boats and pockets as part of the spoils of war; indeed it would
make fascinating research to follow items such as sea chests and
trace how frequently they changed hands!

However, the Official Naval Records of England make
absolutely no references to George Somers serving on any of
these privateering boats during the 1570's, or the 1580's. Likewise, the archives of the Privy Council in London betray no
evidence of his having been granted a Letter of Patent to serve
as a privateer at this time. He could therefore not have worked
as a privateer at this point in his life, as had often been implied.
It may indeed be that he was perhaps an investor in some of
those voyages which resorted to privateering as a lucrative side-
line, without official approval. If he did ever happen to be on such
boats then he may have been aboard as the representative of the
ship's owners—a capacity which basically required that he

catalogue the merchandise which was bought, sold and exchanged during the voyage. Naturally, such a functionary would have had to list any plundered items too, so that they could be accounted for in the documentation required of the authorities at the Prize Court and customs sheds.

There is no doubt that many family fortunes were being made at this time. Privateering had always been the leading source for rapid personal enrichment. People still talked of the amazing haul of plunder which Francisco Pizarro and Diego de Almagro had brought back from Peru in 1533; lowly soldiers on that expedition had reportedly been rewarded with 280 pounds of silver each, plus 4,550 pounds of gold! Officers "according to their degree of calling" had fetched upwards of 30,000 pounds of gold and silver. The Emporer got his customary one-fifth of the total amd messrs. Pizarro and de Almagro took home what was left of the nearly two million pounds of gold and just under a quarter-million pounds of silver. These were not ideal dreams for romantic soothsayers; there was a lot of money to be made from such careers. Even a more moderate haul of say 700 hides worth ten shillings each, or six chests of cochineel weighing 100 lbs. at twenty-six shillings per pound were not to be sneezed at!

But once again, the name of George Somers is missing from all available sources of evidence, prior to 1589. Stephen Hare, Luke Ward, Edward Fenton, Christopher Lister and William Michelson are all easily fingered. But George Somers remains conspicuous by his absence. He doesn't even feature in the extensive shipping survey which the Portuguese government gathered for the years 1572-1587. A most literate gentleman named Lopez Val had been commissioned to compile exhaustive documentation on "English Activities in the Spanish Empire." Just as Richard Hakluyt was doing in England, he had patiently interviewed officers and crew and assembled an authoritive picture of maritime activities for that period.

Actually, Signor Lopez Val had the misfortune to get himself captured, along with his notes, by Robert Witherington in 1586— at which point his research and labours came to an abrupt halt. His information, however, gradually filtered into the public domain, resulting in a hearty mixture of embarrassed blushes, prompt denials and some chest-thumping. It was a tell-all story about Elizabeth's seamen abroad, as seen through the eyes of her foes. Reputations were immediately enhanced by these revelations, or speedily shattered. It was hastily deplored by those who were identified and eagerly enjoyed by those who weren't. But, right up to that final ensnaring moment when this trustworthy scribe was prevented from finishing his last sentence, there was never any mention of a person named Somers as having participated in any battles or skirmishes at this time; not off the Spanish coast, Central America, The Caribbean nor South America.

We must therefore accept that there is nothing whatsoever to link George Somers to privateering, in any form, either directly or indirectly, prior to the 1580's. Quite clearly, whilst he was in his thirties he was married and living at Berne Manor. And his private wealth was based entirely upon his active participation in the same family business which John Somers had started many years before, when he was a mere tradesman in Lyme Regis.

But all of this would soon change. George Somers was about to start undertaking ventures which were entirely of his own chosing. He was establishing an identity which would bring him celebrity status. He and his young wife would soon reap the full rewards of his talents and skills.

7

Armada Intrigue
And The Aftermath

In the annals of naval warfare, few battles have managed to capture the imagination in the way of that fought between the English and Spanish in 1588. Known simply as "The Armada," it pitted champions against champions as two mighty nations sought to claim supreme control of the world's oceans. It was an epic fight between galleons and frigates; powerful boats under full sail chasing one another across the waters, cannon blasting gaping holes into the sides of their massive oaken hulls. It was an event of epic proportions, the type which created instant folk-heroes and spawned tales which became immediate legends.

It had tested them all. Richard Hawkins commanded "Swallow"; John Hawkins was aboard "Victory"; Martin Frobisher was given "Triumph"; John Davis was captain of "Black Dog"; James Lancaster had "Edward Bonaventure." And, if we are to believe folklore, the crew of the boat "Revenge" waited patiently and quietly at anchor off Plymouth Habour whilst the Vice-Admiral of the fleet, Sir Francis Drake, casually completed his game of bowls!

The Spanish Armada had cast off on July 19th. and was ominously becalmed off Portland Bill by 23rd. July. It must have been an impressive and intimidating spectacle, clearly visible from The Cobb at Lyme Regis, on the other side of Lyme Bay. Under the command of the Duke of Medina-Sidona, one hundred-

and-thirty ships had set sail; on board were thirty thousand armed men eager to do battle. From the portals of their collective decks, the Spanish seamen had carefully positioned two thousand-five-hundred cannon of different shapes and sizes—but each charged and ready to blast.

And when their fury finally erupted, the vessels fought their way along the English Channel and chased each other through the North Sea, on around the uppermost tip of Scotland and then down the coast of Ireland. And by October, with nearly three months of continuous combat behind them, there were only sixty-four Spanish ships left to limp southwards, to home once more. The loss of life and vessels had been substantial for both sides but all of those who had fought stood proud and erect. From the most aristocratic of the Captains, to the lowest ranked cabin-boys, they had all served with valour—and none of them would ever forget what it had been like to go to war, at sea. And when the smoke finally cleared and only charred driftwood littered the beaches of England, the inns of her southern shores once again belched freely with the laughter and pride of those who had sailed into Hell, and survived.

But the battle had serious international repercussions too. For Spain, defeat had dealt a devastating blow to the patriotic belief in its own invincibility on the High Seas. For England, victory would provide a generous and welcome boost in confidence. From that moment onwards, her seamen would become the hunters; her captains would no longer cast cautious, furtive glances over their shoulders in fear of the boats of France or Spain. It was now **their** turn to shy away, to cautiously hold back a little; to peer from behind headlands whilst the Royal Fleet drifted brazenly passed. The entire psychology of seafaring had changed, been reversed.

But not all of the country's soldiers and sailors had gone out to sea that summer to face The Armada directly. There were numerous tasks to be carried-out on land. Robert Devereaux, the Earl of Essex, had recently been knighted; he was placed in charge of the Royal Horse Troop and posted near to the mouth of the River Thames, the point at which it was considered that a Spanish landing was most likely to occur. Just a little further up the road, at Tilbury, was stationed the most senior military officer in England, Lieutenant-General Sir Robert Dudley, the Earl of Leicester. Even Lord Howard, as Admiral of the Fleet, was not at sea all of the time, being forced to divide himself between meetings in London and meetings on the poop-deck.

Likewise, Walter Raleigh was given shore duties. He had

already become involved with the development of a policy towards colonisation; he had gone to Virginia several times since 1583 and at the time of The Armada was delicately engaged in securing financial support for a new venture from a group of London merchants. He had been knighted in 1584, was an elected Member of Parliament for Devon and had secured a Royal Patent to sell wine throughout the country. Furthermore, since 1586, he had held three other public offices: Captain of the Queen's Guards, member of the Naval Prize Court and Vice-Admiral of Devon and Cornwall. At the time of The Armada, therefore, Sir Walter was well occupied on land and his talents had been deployed into the logistics of assembling the English fleet.

Using his intimate knowledge of the West Country, its merchants, its sailors and their boats, Raleigh went from town to town trying to amass vessels and crew until each had filled a prescribed quota, and the fleet was ready to leave.

George Somers seems to have been given the same responsibilities in the County of Dorset, where his knowledge of the area and its people could be purposely put to similar use. Lyme Regis contributed boats and men to the English fleet and neighbouring towns did likewise. It was his task to collate statistics and ensure that men and boats were ultimately at anchor when and where they were required. It was relatively easy for him to do and the main problem which he encountered appears to have been in the nature of a squabble over the people of Axminster's reluctance to meet their designated proportionable contributions. He eventually solved this local crisis through the offices of the Privy Council in London.

But George Somers had already played an active, crucial role in this battle of 1588; one which few ever knew about and one which he probably played for several years. The key to this intriguing task lay in the very low-profile visit which had been paid to Lyme Regis as early as 1586 by Sir Francis Walsingham, the Queen's senior and most trusted advisor. Ostensibly he had arrived in order to compile a report for Her Majesty on the very serious storm which the town had experienced the previous winter.

In reality, Sir Francis Walsingham was Elizabeth's spymaster, a man around whom a web of secrecy had been gently woven for many years; it is inconceivable that when this exulted visitor arrived in Lyme Regis in 1586, his attention was devoted solely to inspecting storm damage. Why then had he come?

Francis Walsingham's network of spies reached deeply into

the foreign diplomatic corps of Europe and had infiltrated religious and regal circles alike. His agents were both overt and covert operatives, skilled men and women from whom virtually no information could ever be regarded as sacred.

As early as 1585 troubling fragments had started to reach his ears concerning an unusual build-up of the conventional Spanish fleet; in response, Walsingham promptly spread his cloak and unleashed a small army of proven agents. One of them was a mysterious lady code-named Maude, a lady who enjoyed what were discretely referred to as "intimately close ties" to the Court of the Spanish Ambassador to France. Also activated was an ordained Venetian priest then living in Rome; a gentleman who reputedly read the Pope's own private correspondence whilst His Holiness was asleep! Another agent known as Sutton was dispatched to Genoa, where he quickly learnt that an extensive fund-raising programme was underway, directly aimed at providing the finances for the preparation of men and ammunition. An Armada was clearly being outfitted for an attack against England in early 1587. Walsingham received this confirmation soon after January 1586.

The highly sensitive nature of this information resulted in the Queen allowing Walsingham himself to embark on a nationwide fact-finding mission of the country's ports. He needed to assess the Nation's state of readiness should Spain subsequently decide to attack in early summer of the following year. What he discovered was neither encouraging nor gratifying and he was compelled to take drastic and urgent measures to prevent this Armada from leaving on schedule. In short, his agents provided sufficient details and maps for the Queen to authorise Sir Francis Drake to set sail for Cadiz and annihilate whatever of the fleet the Spanish had managed to assemble. Caught completely off-guard, the nucleus of the Armada was thrashed and its departure was subsequently delayed until 1588, when the English themselves would be more conveniently ready!

In light of these behind-the-scene activities of Sir Francis Walsingham, we must therefore scrutinise his apparently innocuous visit to Lyme Regis in 1586, for it clearly had far more profound motives than to merely inspect storm damage. His prime objective was plainly to gather information about local defenses and the availability of ships and men from the area around Lyme. He was afterall compiling the secret report which eventually resulted in firm evasive action being taken to prevent the pending Spanish attack for 1587. Lyme was an ideal place to begin his assessment because this had always been the port from which patrols were dispatched for a quick reconnoitre for Spanish galleons. Even a century later the Mayor of Lyme Regis is on record as having sent a ship out to The Scilly Isles, in order to check and see whether there were any foreign boats moving in and around the mouth of the English Channel.

Since George Somers had a major role in the acquisition of logistical information, when The Armada **did** arrive in 1588, then he was certainly among that tight group of informants who spoke with Walsingham on his previous visit. The spy-master had agents such as him all over the country, persons who could furnish precise up-to-date details at critical times; individuals whose collective data gave substance to the moulding of official policies, and dictated military strategy. Sir Francis was curiously inept when it came to taking notes and minutes of such meetings; the names of those in this coterie were rarely placed on paper! Therefore, there was never an official record of this aspect of his visit to Lyme Regis in 1586; but we do know that he met with a group of the town's leading citizens and was assured that twenty-three seaworthy ships would be on hand for the Queen's defensive fleet in 1588. George Somers was certainly in the group, although in the words of the Public Records Offices, in London, ". . . you may never piece it together . . .!"

With all of these matters off his chest, Walsingham then felt free to return to the pressing business of ensnaring Mary Queen of Scots, an irritating little matter which had already occupied too much time for both himself and Queen Elizabeth. After successfully managing to infiltrate an agent named Giffard into Mary's innermost household staff, the master sleuth was able to tap, read and redirect her private mail as best befitted his needs. The tired monarch from across the border soon tripped and stumbled into all manner of traps and trickery. At eight o'clock on the morning of February 8th. 1587, she was beheaded—and Sir Francis Walsingham was then able to concentrate more fully on The Armada of 1588.

Throughout that Spring he received a steady flow of information from Richard Hakluyt, who was then serving as a diplomatic aide in Paris. Hakluyt, later destined to become a business associate of George Somers, obligingly reported all of his conversations with his Portuguese counterpart Loao de Castro, back to Walsingham in London. As a reward, he received Sir Francis' personal patronage, a prestigeous advantage which enabled him to devote his time to researching his classic book "Principal Navigations."

This was therefore the intriguing backdrop which lay behind

The Armada as it sat becalmed off Portland Bill on that fateful 23rd. July 1588. George Somers was among those who gathered along The Cobb to watch it drifting on the opposite side of Lyme Bay. Sadly, not everyone could join the foray. Many, like him had to be content with contributing from the shore. And when it was all over three months later and they had returned to the more mundane chores of daily life, the majority would never be aware of the true role which George Somers had played during the preceeding years—covertly feeding nautical data to Sir Francis Walsingham. And when the highly detailed list containing "The Names of Her Majesties ships, and others that served" was compiled on 13th. December 1588, it would only silently reveal that George Somers had not put to sea.

Whilst Somers looked at the passing Armada, his gaze may perhaps have crossed that of its Commander-in-Chief, the Duke of Medina-Sidona. At that moment he was reportedly still thinking about a large house which he had noticed on a hill in Plymouth; having captured London, he planned to march victoriously westwards, through Lyme Regis, and would then use that same big, white house as his own private retreat. However, like so many other things in the life of this well-intentioned Spanish nobleman, that would never be. With charisma and misfortune his career had slipped and slithered as one crossing the muddy plains on the family seat outside Seville. It was he who had been in charge of Cadiz when Drake had destroyed the fleet in 1587— and then behaved like a true gentleman when Drake returned ten days later to impertinently ask for provisions! The Armada of 1588 proved to be one of the crowning flops for this otherwise pleasant and friendly man.

In the aftermath of the battle, England assumed a more aggressive stance and in the years which followed, her seamen regularly headed off to settle old scores and make war.

For her part, the Queen had become far more receptive to the proponents of colonisation; the advantages to be gained from establishing colonies had become appealing. There had been a lot of active interest in the West Country related to colonisation, especially since 11th. June 1578 when Sir Humphrey Gilbert had been granted a license to start colonising. Since 1583, both Raleigh and Sir Richard Grenville had made significant and practical inroads in trying to settle the area around Roanoke Island—which they had named "Virginia" in honour of their supposedly virgin Queen.

George Somers had met regularily with both men and had been with them as recently as March 1588, when they gathered to inspect a real-live Indian whom Grenville had recently brought back from The Americas. Joy abounded when their "savage guest" agreed to be baptised in Bideford, Devon—although regrettably, he was not sufficiently blessed, for he died four months later . . . as the Spanish Armada was entering the English Channel.

During the next decade George Somers became increasingly more visible as England confirmed her domination of the seas. He became directly involved in many of the major sea-battles which were to be fought and he emerged with a proven reputation as both a seaman and a military leader.

The first of these opportunities arose in 1589 when he was assigned to the vessel "Flibcoate" for an expedition down to Portugal and The Azores. There were several important voyages that year and between April 1st. and December they became confusingly interwoven.

Confident at having just soundly rumped Spain, Elizabeth next ordered that Drake and Sir John Norris should embark on a trip to Portugal with the intention of placing Don Antonio atop the Portuguese throne, as a replacement for his arch-rival Prince Philip. The heir-presumptive was vigorously favoured by, naturally enough, Spain. With the help of some Dutch boats, a fleet estimated at 150 boats and 23,000 men was assembled at Plymouth and then headed southwards. In the middle of the Bay of Biscay they were joined by the small flotilla of the Earl of Essex. Having been forced to sit out the last major battle with a group of horsemen, at the mouth of the River Thames, this eager Earl was veritably straining at the bit for full-bloodied action. After reaching Portuguese waters, Essex was landed with the bulk of the infantry and musketmen at Peniche, whilst Drake and Norris headed up the Tagus, for Lisbon.

The English were genuinely driven by the belief that the people of Portugal "should not be in slavery under a stranger, deprived of their natural King," but they appear to have backed the wrong horse. Don Antoio's claim to the throne evidently rested upon his being the illegitimate son of King Henry of Portugal—how that qualified him in the eyes of moralistic England is hard to imagine, unless it was payment for having been another of Walsingham's agents! Anyhow, the assault did not produce the anticipated popular uprising expected and their earlier optimism soon crumbled with inadequate food and ammunition. A post mortem of the failure also revealed that another contributary factor was that many soldiers became "drunke with the plentie of wines."

The fleet headed back for England in angered disarray, with many of them scattering to plunder villages along the coast. It was reported that in several they were found Spanish soldiers and sailors who were still making their weary ways back from the slaughter of The Armada. As the dispirited rabble moved homewards they pillaged, robbed and burnt; prisoners were taken and, according to Captain Richard Wingfield, others had "their throates cut." In early June, some of them encountered two small barkes which were carrying "victuals" for the main fleet. The broken fleet stocked-up and many went to England; others replenished their supplies and headed for more privateering in The Azores, with the Earl of Essex.

On 2nd. July Drake and Norris returned to Plymouth where many of the soldiers were paid only five shillings for their troubles in the fruitless disaster. Essex took his boats to the island of San Miguel where, on August 1st he was joined by a small fleet under the command of the Earl of Cumberland.

Cumberland's party consisted of four boats, among which was the one commanded by Captain Pigeon, with George Somers on board. With him were "several gentlemen" from Plymouth and also the noted mathematician and engineer Edward Wright—alias "Captain Careless" from when he had captained "Hope" on a previous trip to Santo Domingo with Francis Drake. Soon afterwards, they were joined by Captain Amayas Preston and his ships.

This informal congregation of galleons, carvels, barkes and frigates proved to be highly rewarding. They captured a boat from Puerto Rico, carrying sugar, ginger and hides; another from Africa laden with elephant teeth, grains, coconuts and goat hides. Preston took one from the West Indies loaded with sugar; Cumberland's fleet captured a Portuguese ship on its way back from Brazil with rare wood, more sugar and hides.

By the time that they eventually turned towards England in November, they had captured an estimated 60 to 91 prize-boats and their decks were dangerously bulging with a stunning quantity of booty and prisoners—so much, that it was felt that some of the ships might sink under the weight. They had even snatched a French fishing boat, quietly making its way back across the Atlantic from Newfoundland with its catch of cod.

"Flibcoate" was similarily bursting with its share of gold, ivory, spices, cloths, hides and prisoners. Very gingerly she sailed around Ram Head, the Cape just west of Plymouth, and then skirted the craggy rock at Edy Stone off Plymouth Sound. Because Falmouth harbour was only seventeen feet deep at low tide, George Somers and his fellow crew decided not to risk running aground on the sandy bottom and, instead, made for Dartmouth.

The entire venture had more than adequately compensated for the misery felt at having so disasterously failed with Don Anotonio some months earlier. George Somers was indeed about to share in a substantial treasure trove. The Naval Prize Court, with Walter Raleigh as one of its members, placed a worth of eight-thousand pounds on the plunder which was aboard "Flibcoate"; the total worth of the prize boats, gold and silver which other vessels had claimed boggles the mind!

Once the spoils had been fairly divided, Somers made his way back home to Lyme Regis. After conducting some business through his brother Nicholas, he then took a horse and rode out to Berne Manor where his wife was awaiting his arrival. Then, in true Elizabethan fashion, they quickly agreed to invest his share of the proceeds in buying more land.

This had been the first proven privateering trip made by George Somers. It had quenched his thirst, but his mouth was still left dry for more.

8

The Quieter Years

Following his triumphant return from The Azores in 1589, so resplendent with the treasure-bulging holds of "Flibcoate," George Somers was then quite unexpectedly destined to pass the better part of the next five years almost permanently fixed to the land. In some respects, this quiet phase of his life has provoked as much controversy and misunderstanding as have his more active and hectic years. This is mainly because many find it difficult to reconcile the image of a robust seaman with that of a placid country squire sitting contentedly among the green, rolling hillsides of Dorset.

Much of this conflict stems from the purely anecdotal sketch of George Somers which was provided by the seventeenth century preacher, writer and scholar Thomas Fuller (1601-1661). It was he who first gave birth to the oft-quoted cliche about Somers being ". . . a lion at sea . . . and a lamb on land . . ." This colourful turn of words appeared in his book "The History of the Worthies," a document actually published by his son shortly after Fuller had died. The writer was a man noted above all else for his anecdotes and quaintness of literary style and, by his own admission, Mr. Fuller never laid claims to having conducted "any profound research and wrote far too many books." Such a description can therefore hardly be treated as particularly accurate, but must be taken instead as nothing more than an amusing thumb-sketch. Fuller himself never intended for it to be taken either literally or seriously, otherwise we might have to start looking for **other** traits of this implied schizophrenia.

Lamentably, Fuller's description has become the breeding ground for numerous other references to George Somers, each apparently eager to use it as an authorative rubber stamp with which to explain subsequent actions and events in his life.

It has been argued that George Somers was more-or-less obliged to spend some time at home as a quasi-country squire, in order to satisfy his wife, a tolerant lady who was forced to spend too much time on her own out at Berne Manor. But this is pure nonsense! She had married him knowing that he was a merchant-adventurer and therefore likely to spend much time away from her; furthermore, she had been partially raised in the country and was probably far happier there than in the town. There is absolutely nothing to substantiate that Joane was likely to have hen-pecked or nagged her husband into staying behind. Like her contemporaries, she knew only too well what her place and functions were to be and she was doubtless quite elated to have married a man who could provide her with such an impressive and increasing trove of riches.

Equally as absurd are the peculiar ramblings of F. J. Pope who seeks to explain this particular period of George Somers' life by remarking that "the enriched sea-captain attempted to live the life of a country gentleman and he failed to appreciate it ..."

The simple, uncomplicated truth is that from late 1589 until 1594 George Somers became land-based as a direct result of personal choice and family circumstances.

It must be fully understood that ambitious men who sought wealth and respectability in Elizabethan England could only lay serious claim to either, by investing in land. Unless they were of aristocratic stock, the most that many could aspire to was to become one of the establishment, by joining the landed-gentry. The quest to have "gentleman" affixed behind the name on public documents was no petty ego-trip. It was a serious goal and one which George Somers now shared with countless others. Like them, he therefore invested heavily in real estate.

Through his marriage to Joane, he had acquired three tenements in Lyme Regis, although this did not genuinely qualify as being "his." It was not until 1587 that he had begun to acquire property in his own right. That year he bought the life-lease on land at Whitchurch Canonicorum and also the 200 acres of farmland at Berne, "complete with the Manor house thereon." This latter transaction had cost him six-hundred pounds. Next, using his share from the "Flibcoate" expedition of 1589, he secured the far more impressive estate of eleven-hundred-and-sixty acres at Upwey. It consisted of extensive farmland, several buildings, at least two mills and a manor called "Waybayhouse." In a subsequent deed dated 31st. August 1671, which retrospectively refers to the estate of "the late Sir George Somers," there is also mention of a farm called "Voway"—which may have been part of the same transactions for Upwey which he began to negotiate in 1589.

It is obvious that George and Joane Somers had previously been discussing the acquisition of the Upwey property before he actually had the funds to pay for it, because legal documents had already been drawn-up within weeks of his return from The Azores. These preliminary overtures had been made through Hugh Keate. He was one of the principals involved with this enormous holding, but he died soon after April 16th. 1590 and George Somers thereafter found himself involved in considerable legal complications which incorporated several executors and trustees—each of whom was desperately trying to sort-out the transfer of leases and partnerships connected with the property.

But in addition to expanding his land-ownership, two other events happened which made George accept responsibilities and commitments away from the sea. Both concerned deaths within the family.

Firstly, at the beginning of 1590 his brother Nicholas unexpectedly died. We have no medical records to provide the cause of death and, in a way, it is not directly relevent. The true significance to George Somers was that the eldest of the three brothers—the one who had taken charge of the family business—was now dead. Such a critical void had to be filled immediately, otherwise their combined lifelong efforts would collapse, to no avail. (By this time, John Somers senior was already dead, although no record can be located to provide a date.) George would have to step into his place even if only on a temporary basis.

There were other ramifications too, to Nicholas' death. He had left a widow and two small sons: Nicholas, aged ten, and Matthew then aged eight. Having no children of their own, George and Joane readily undertook to take care of them.

Within one single year, they had acquired substantial land-holdings, unexpected business obligations and a second family. On its own, the effective management of their estates would require considerable time and expertise, because the Upwey property involved transferring and handling the leases of some acreage to farmers, under existing agreements. Located some miles from Berne at Weymouth, this would make additional travelling necessary. There were out-buildings to be rented and grazing permits to be issued. Now, on top of this, he had the prospects of having to handle an active import-export business, plus the needs of two nephews and a sister-in-law to take care of. At that moment the outlook must have looked ominous indeed!

Furthermore, shortly after Nicholas had died, there was another emotional hurdle to stumble across. At some point in the Spring of 1590 his mother passed away. Alice Somers had been living with her sister Thomasine for several years, sharing her home "The Cleeves," in Lyme. They had been two elderly ladies enjoying life with walks through the town and happily pottering their way through the gardened parts of the eight acres which surrounded the house. They were no trouble to anyone. Of Thomasine's life we have no descriptions, but we can surely assume that Alice's three sons ensured that they wanted for nothing; John and Nicholas had both continued to reside in Lyme Regis and would have paid them regular visits. When George and Joane were in town they too would have popped in to visit his mother and aunt. The Somers family had always been close, each member responding to the needs of the others. The three brothers had grown-up as friends; now, with families of their own, John and George found themselves alone, shouldering the joys and burdens which the family had produced in a lifetime.

Several key relationships grew from this tragic year. In order to help him cope with the questions of property, George surrendered most of these responsibilities to a gentleman named Baldwin Sandford. He was a neighbour out at Whitchurch and may already have been renting some of the Somers land around Berne for his own use. In any event, Baldwin Sandford became the estate-manager for George and Joane Somers, handling farmland and orchards associated with Berne Manor and Marshwood. The more complicated administration of distant Upwey remained under the care of the management team who were dealing with it prior to his ownership.

A second relationship which emerged from this series of bereavements was that which he developed with John Gould, a merchant from Dorchester, the County's main town. Gould had his own family, with sons involved with his business in much the same way that the Somers boys had worked alongside their father as youths. Between them, George and John Somers must have come to various sub-contractual and financial agreements with the Goulds, for the name frequently occurs in dealings which concerned one party of the other after 1590. (It so happens, that even in George's will he makes specific references to the settlement of outstanding debts due to this same John

Gould of Dorchester.) Furthermore, Gould had a son named Nicholas who subsequently became quite active in London money markets at the turn of the century; as George Somers gravitated more towards the city, he and Nicholas may well have benefitted from mutual contacts.

Finally, the death of Nicholas Somers meant the start of a very close relationship between George and his nephew Matthew. It may have been that Matthew was the more wayward of the two and therefore required more of their uncle's attention; perhaps it was simply that they shared a common love for the sea. No matter whatever it was which kindled the initial sparks, they evolved a closeness which resulted in Matthew being at George Somers' side right up to the time that he died; and Matthew became a main beneficiary in his will.

Although there was no reason to presume that he was not just as favourably inclined toward the other nephew, Matthew and George Somers grew much closer together—not that there should be anything suspicious or surprising about this. It was regarded as being quite dreadful if a married couple were childless in Elizabethan Times, particularily so if the husband had any public standing; for a seaman it was doubly embarrassing.

Whereas the churches did not have any special doctrine to actually condemn such unfortunates the superstitious tone of the period was quite fertile with ghastly explanations to account for it. It was taken for granted that there was some unpleasant physical problem at the root cause—perhaps they had had The Plague and this was a side-effect. Was it an omen of Evil? The manifestation of a dreadful secret which neither party had been willing to confess? Was there a skeleton hidden somewhere in the cupboard? A curse? A scourge? Witches had not yet become the whipping post for public doubts and suspicions, but childless, married couples were clearly vulnerable to all manner of gossip!

Actually, it seems that probably Joane was barren.

Couples without a natural heir invariably sought to acquire one, so that the legal passage of any inheritance might proceed with an orderly and predetermined line of succession. For this reason it was not at all unusual for a nephew to be "adopted" and groomed to become the beneficiary of the will. When Nicholas Somers died it therefore became fairly automatic that the youngest of his sons should be brought closer to his uncle; the eldest brother had already become their father's heir.

For the four years after 1590, George Somers efficiently acted his various roles with different hats; he was a business man, a surrogate father and a country squire. Simultaneously he became more involved with the local people—the farmers, the merchants, the Guild, the Town Council. He came to learn about the politics of Lyme Regis and set this into a perspective which incorporated the country as a whole.

However, on the clearest of days, from Berne Manor he could always catch that glimpse of the sea and vivid pictures of The Cobb and boats would rush back into his mind. They could not have escaped the thoughts of the owner of Berne Manor too often.

By 1594, he was already being wooed by Walter Raleigh to join him on an exciting expedition across the Atlantic and down into South America. He was assured by his friend that when they ventured up the rivers of Guiana they would find the legendary city of El Dorado, "The City of Gold!" It was an adventure which must have been hard to turn-down and the prospects must have tormented George Somers for several months, dominating conversations with his wife and brother—and perhaps even with young Matthew. Raleigh had also approached another of their mutual friends—Amayas Preston. But neither man went, that year.

General domestic circumstances, however, had gradually begun to resolve themselves and in early 1595 George Somers once more prepared to set sail.

He left Berne Manor, rode cross-country through Charmouth and entered Lyme Regis. After conversing with John and assuring himself that Nicholas' widow and her children were correctly taken care of, he made ready to head for the Caribbean. It would be a voyage to make history.

9

♛♛♛♛♛♛♛♛♛♛♛♛♛♛♛♛♛♛♛♛♛♛♛

Into Battle—1595

♟♟♟♟♟♟♟♟♟♟♟♟♟♟♟♟♟♟♟♟♟♟♟♟♟

Since its resounding defeat in 1588, Spain had desperately tried to cling onto whatever it could salvage from its tattered reputation. Her home ports were being consistently bombarded; her frigates were attacked, chased, robbed and sunk. On the far side of the Atlantic her once majestic Empire looked forlornly towards the horizon, waiting for the masts and flags of England; expecting to be attacked by her relentless adversary.

In 1595, the onslaught was to continue. Drake and Hawkins were in Plymouth finalising arrangements for a major military campaign later in the year; one which would cloud the skies of The West Indies with smoke, fill the air with burning fumes and colour The Caribbean Sea with the rich hues of blood.

During the year, as many as one hundred English ships would eventually cross the Atlantic. In February, Walter Raleigh took a fleet of five boats to South America, as part of his ongoing quest to find "The City of Gold." In March, George Somers and Amayas Preston set sail.

Somers and Preston had sailed together before and had been friends since the mid-eighties. Their voyage was one of obvious privateering using a Royal licence which Elizabeth had granted Captain Preston some years earlier. They had three boats with them. Preston was on "Ascension"; George Somers commanded "The Gift" and a smaller pinnance guarded the rear. They had originally intended to depart from Plymouth at about the same time as Raleigh but were delayed whilst they awaited the arrival of their consort vessels—"Derling," under Captain Jones and

"Angel," with Captain Prowse at the helm. In the end, George Somers and Amayas Preston left on 12th. March and Jones followed a week later, on 19th. March.

They took the customary route along the coasts of Spain and Portugal and then headed for The Canary Islands; from here they could more-or-less go with the ocean currents all the way into The Caribbean. Another advantage of the route was that it offered the off-chance that they might be able to snatch a Spanish prize on the way through—a temptation which none could resist.

It was, in fact, in this spirit that Captain Preston suddenly took-off under full-sail shortly after sighting silhouettes of the distant islands—and began chasing what he took to be an enemy frigate, to the east. Somers watched him go and gently changed course into The Canaries. Captain Preston, however, was soon given the slip by his prey, but with pulses already beating excitedly, he altered his tack and made for the island of Puerto Santo—a semi-retirement centre for elderly Portuguese soldiers, just north of Madeira. There, somewhat before dawn on March 31st. he landed sixty of his men and had them take refuge from the rain in a wayside chapel, until it was light enough for them to see what they were doing. By the end of the day they had thrashed the startled geriatrics, chased men, women and children through thickets and bushes, and burnt their town "utterly to the ground."

In the interim, George Somers was still prowling the archipelago looking for him. On 6th. April he unexpectedly made contact with the delayed Captain Jones on "Derling"; and a couple of days later they joined forces with another three English vessels which were anchored to the south-east of Grand Canary. Among their leaders were Captains Hampton and Willis. Finally they caught sight of Amayas Preston, calmly at anchor off Gomera Island, licking his wounded pride and bemoaning the meagre spoils which the side-trip had brought.

Once reunited with Preston, they all decided to form a convoy and travel together to The West Indies. Three weeks later the crews were bathing in the warm waters off the coast of Dominica, trading with the natives for bananas, potatoes and pineapples, in exchange for knives, hatchets and that familiar stand-by—beads! They stayed here until May 14th., replenishing their food and water supplies, whilst Captain Preston gave his men the chance to recover from their various injuries, the souvenirs of Puerto Santo.

From here they sailed south-west and glided along the shores of Grenada, eyes forever alert for signs that Spaniards might be in the area; eager to seek them out for combat. On they went, among the cays of The Testigos Islands before eventually dropping anchor off The Margaritas.

It was well-known that Spanish sailors frequently traded here and paid the natives to go diving for pearls. It was a likely spot to encounter the enemy. As soon as they arrived, the islanders greeted them from dug-out canoes and hastily offered to pay a voluntary ransom providing that Somers and Preston would promise not to invade their peaceful homeland. The offer was readily accepted. Then, on the night of 19th. May, they quietly slipped over to the beaches of tiny Coche Island and waited.

Their patience and vigilance were hardly well-rewarded. Over the next few days they wiled away the hours by diving-up a handful of pearls; they fished for mullets and even had the incredible experience of hauling in an eighteen foot Cayman crocodile. But it was well below their expectations. Other than a few Spanish drifters with their slaves, they did not find any signs of a larger patrol of ships. Somewhat disgruntled, they stole three boats laden with salted bacon and maize and travelled on.

Their next port-of-call was Cumana, a Spanish colony on the north coast of South America. Cumana had actually been the first settlement which Spain had established in the region—in 1523—but none of the sailors was remotely concerned with this scrap of historical irrelevance. Their only interest was to successfully loot and burn the town. They had no time to dally in aesthetics and learning.

The capture of Cumana was accomplished with relative ease, although when they managed to sit-down in the main market square, they realised that the retreating soldiers had also retreated with the luckless Captain Willis and six of his men firmly in tow. (For Willis, it would mean a patient wait of one year before the parishioners back home in England had managed to collect enough to cover his ransom demand!)

At this moment they decided that having come thus far, they should press further around the rim of the Spanish Empire and cast a blow closer to its heart. They smashed the fortifications of Cumana, wrecked its buildings and created havoc among the burning houses which lined its cobbled streets. Then, once safely again on their boats, they sailed westwards.

By the evening of May 26th. they were anchored in the bay off La Guayra but rough seas prevented any landing until the following morning. At first light, George Somers dispatched an unarmed deputation to meet the resident commander of the garrison. It was a courtesy, intended to advise the local authorities of an imminent attack and giving them the option of avoiding it by paying a ransom. It practice, it was a seafarers' way of throwing down the gauntlet because no self-respecting officer could refuse a challenge. We know nothing of the terms which were proposed, only that they were clearly too absurd to be paid. They all readied for battle.

Their specific target was not this small defensive outpost, but a far grander prize further inland, up in the mountains. Spain had controlled Venezuela since Alonzo de Ojeda first reached Maracaibo in 1499. In fact the sight of stilted native villages on the coastline reminded him of Venice and he had therefore named in Venezuela, "little Venice." After settling at Cumana, the Spaniards had constructed their next most important town at a place which they named Santiago de Leon de Caracas. It was here that George Somers had decided to give "la muerte"—the death blow.

This mountain town had originally been founded in 1560 but the indigenous Caracas Indians soon destroyed it. The persistent Spaniards had subsequently re-established it in 1567 and Caracas had become a thriving town—the gateway for future ambitions which they still had to thrust deeper into South America.

Venezuela is a mountainous country, where steep rock faces spill abruptly onto a narrow coastal strip and then plunge into the sea. For George Somers it evoked memories of the Dorset shoreline; another sailor mentioned that it reminded him of the peaked islands of The Canary Islands. The first line of defence was the garrison at La Guayra, after which the Spaniards had somewhat limply relied upon the precipitous terrain to defend the rest of the countryside.

George Somers' preliminary assault team landed on the beach east of the main fort and then entered the garrison with little resistance. The bulk of the troopers had long since fled and their Governor was found fast asleep in the nearby woods. He was brought back and interrogated, before being put aboard Captain Preston's ship for safe keeping. He revealed very little, except to note that the invaders had been expected for over a month, during which all roads into Caracas had become firmly barricaded and secured; he warned them that there were ambushes ready in all ravines; trees had been felled across all entrances.

Following a brief rest, during which time they corralled prisoners and ferried small quantities of booty out to their boats in the bay, the main body of English infantrymen was ready to begin the climb up to Santiago de Leon de Caracas. George

Somers had had the foresight to question a native Indian about other ways of reaching the town and from him it was learnt that other older routes did exist, dating from pre-colonial days. The man was hired as their guide.

George Somers and Amayas Preston led their troops along narrow cattle paths, climbing among thorny bushes and shrubs; they cut their way through abundant glades of rhododendrums and worked along winding, precipitous goat trails. Higher and higher they went. There are some excellent descriptions of their hard trek—as seamen, unused to back-packing and climbing rock faces, slipped and fell; were cut, bruised and became exhausted. The skin of their palms had become hardened by pulling at oars and tugging at ropes, but their fingers were not accustomed to gripping sharp rocks, nor probing craggy crevices. The tips became cut and bloodied; climbing became more awkward. The soldiers often fared no better; the more seasoned pike and musketmen had been retained for the Drake and Hawkins expedition; these were younger, less experienced. They too began to tire. The heat hovered constantly in the eighties and although this was the start of the wet season, intermittent showers and occasional off-shore breezes did little to cool their bodies.

Finally they reached the crest at the Pass de la Venta, and a little higher up they stood at the top of the highest peaks in the vicinity. With brilliant stategy, George Somers had led his men way up to the Silla de Caracas, at an altitude of 8,531 feet. Beneath them lay Caracas, the fabled "City of Eternal Spring."

The panoramic vistas must have temporarily caused the men to forget their personal discomforts. It was indeed a spectacular sight; orange-topped buildings with white walls, neatly set-out in an orderly square pattern; the entire city comfortably nestled in a basin encircled by steeply rising mountain sides. But this was not the time to enjoy scenery. The men who Somers and Preston had led to those breath-taking heights were eager to get about their task.

It was raining heavily and two-and-a-half months had passed since they had left home—but when they finally got the signal to charge, such thoughts and fatigue were quickly lost to screams and screeches. Muskets fired intermittent volleys; swords clattered and pikemen yelled. Groups of bewildered Caracas Indians stood on the hillsides and watched, joined by roaming patrols of Spanish soldiers who became startled spectators, mesmerised, watching in total dismay this sodden spectacle of English abandonment.

Just as he had led his men up the mountains, so George Somers was at their head when they charged into the town. The carefully-assembled lines of cannon, trenches and soldiers had all been firmly fixed to face the sea—none had expected to be attacked like this from above and behind. The defenders had proved to be totally ill-equipped to handle such a bizarre onslaught. People darted in panic and confusion through the cobbled streets, hoping for guidance from the armed militia which had always protected them; but there was no comfort to be offered that day. Somers led one flank and Amayas Preston took another as they swept through the town centre of Casco. Pandemonium was rife among the scattering residents, as they charged one way and then another in a desperate bid to escape their near-maniacal attackers. Fires burnt out of control, their owners standing by in helpless confusion.

It was indeed incredible that those who had so recently lain in utter exhaustion after the arduous climb up to the Silla, had been so instantly refreshed by the thought of battle; aching limbs, cuts and sprains had no place for those who captured Santiago de Leon de Caracas that day. By late afternoon the city lay in ruins. Homes had been ransacked and remnants of food, drink and pleasure lay discarded alongside the broken furniture which littered the streets.

Civilians had been caught in the steely crossfire, but the main targets had been military; these were now totally destroyed. Barracks smouldered uselessly along the lip of the rim which was supposed to have ensured their protection. And in the distance, the victorious men of George Somers could see the blue sea of the Caribbean. Somewhere down there lay their ships, flying the flags of England. They had suffered only limited losses and the soldiers under Captains Harvey, Roberts and Jones were basically unscathed.

They remained in Caracas from May 29th. until June 3rd. hassling over a final ransom; but Preston's demand for 30,000 ducets was not met. He ordered the town to be stripped of any valuables and it was burnt to ashes. By the morning of June 5th. their loaded boats had sailed away.

On the way back northwards, George Somers was sent to attack three Spanish boats known to be lying at Checherebiche, on the mainland shores. But when he got there he found that the cunning Spanish sailors had shrewdly taken their sails from their boats and hidden them somewhere inland. The vessels could be of no value to him now. But Somers reciprocated the gesture by burning the ships—and left the startled crews sitting on the beaches clutching their sails. He didn't wait to watch them deciding how to get back to Spain, with canvas alone!

By June 20th. they lay at anchor in the Bay of Lagua, in Hispaniola and used the time for rest and recovery free from the pressures of war. Next they journeyed to Jamaica. At this point Captain Hampton took his ships and bade farewell; Captain Jones also left them "to discover some secret matter." (What that matter was we shall not know, for he and his entire crew perished.) There now only remained the three original boats which had left from Plymouth.

They sailed to the Cayman Islands, fished for a while and then rounded the Cape de Corrientes before dropping anchor once more. They were now by Cape St. Anthony, western Cuba, and it was in this remote secluded spot that they met-up with Walter Raleigh, fresh from his trip to Guyana. The date was July 13th. 1595.

For the next week, the two crews exchanged stories and reported on what had happened during their respective travels. But it was Raleigh's men who had the most to talk about; they had been far up the Orinoco River, deep into the hinterland of a mysterious country. Captain Keymis described the muddy delta of the river, one which had so many inlets that initially they couldn't decide which was the real main river. And he told of the Orinoco being so gigantic that at one point there was an island twenty miles long, in the middle of the river itself! Somers and his men listened in awe as Captains Thyn, Calfield and Douglas spoke of richly coloured parrots, macaws and cockatoos continuously circling overhead; and they spoke of monkeys, jaguars, toucans, alligators—and a fish with long teeth which could eat men's flesh and which the natives called "parea."

It all made fascinating listening and George Somers might even have felt a slight twinge of envy, knowing that he had been invited to go along with them.

Their losses had been small both in ships and in men; few had died. Captain Gifford, in fact, disclosed that they had deliberately left his own manservant behind as a gesture of good faith to the chief of one of the tribes. They intended to return the following year and collect the learned Francis Sparrow; however, this was not to be. Due to circumstances beyond his control, Raleigh did not get back to Guyana for another twenty years—at which stage the resilient Mr. Sparrow was discovered to be uselessly fluent in divers native languages and customs! (What a loyal, splendid Sparrow!)

It had all made interesting conversation, but when Preston

and Somers heard Raleigh talking about three foot lizards, serpents and ants which cut leaves, they became sceptical. And when he referred to a creature called "manatee" and claimed that it was really a mermaid, they presumably felt that poor Walter had been in the tropics far too long! (Alas! these same stories were treated with humour on the streets of London and the enthusiastic Raleigh proved unable to secure backers for another trip to search for the elusive El Dorado.)

On July 20th. both groups parted company and headed for England. George Somers chose the northern route. They passed among the islands of The Bahamas, entered the Bahamian Channel and then went north with the Gulf Stream. It was a route which took him for the first confirmed time past Bermuda, the place where he would eventually die.

We know that George Somers was in Bermudian waters by about August 14th. because this was the track which was usually used. Spanish documents specifically directed that their boats should leave Havana, "come out of the channel then thou shalt be at 20 degrees and go north-east until thou be in 39½ degrees and then go north of The Bermudas." Several English accounts of trips back from the West Indies confirm this as their usual pathway. One, by a Captain Hen, says "we left Havana and we disembarqued and came along the islands of Bermuda and crossed over to The Banke and from here sayled for England . . ." Raleigh himself had referred to passing this way many times and warned that "the Bermudas are a hellish area for thunder, lightning and storms . . ."

Unquestionably George Somers came by The Bermudas that month in 1595. They skirted the eastern end, perhaps even heard the eery screeches of the birds which had caused some seamen to call them "The Isles of Devils." They then continued northwards, to fish for a while off The Grand Banks before making the last stage of their journey across to England. Against contrary winds, they berthed in Milford Haven on September 10th. The trip had lasted for nearly six months.

Now they could settle-down to enjoy the spoils of war.

10

Battles At Sea

During the early months of 1596, George Somers continued to bask in considerable public adoration for the prominent role which he had played in the attack against Caracas the previous year. To he and Joane it must have seemed that recognition for their mutual trials and tribulations had finally arrived. They were the talk of Lyme Regis, highly respected throughout the entire county of Dorset and increasingly in demand among the socialities and courtiers in London.

But the euphoric mood of the Nation became one of gloom, almost overnight. Word was received that both Sir Francis Drake and Sir John Hawkins were dead. England reeled under the shock.

Their expeditionary force to The West Indies had optimistically sailed on 28th. August 1595. It consisted of twenty-seven ships and roughly 2,500 men. It was a true "armament," as such warfaring fleets were termed, and was the largest of its kind to have ever crossed the Atlantic under Royal sanction. Now, barely eight months later, the survivors from this impressive show were limping home without significant glory or plunder—able to offer only the skimpiest tales of sporadic encounters with the Spanish, to boost their own morale. The fate of their distinguished leaders soon became clear. Sir John Hawkins had died on November 12th. 1595, after falling sick with a depression and what was called "a broken heart," following several failed attacks. He had been bewildered at the way in which the Spaniards were always waiting for them and he had the firm conviction that they had been pre-warned by spies. He died off Puerto Rico.

Sir Francis Drake died from a bout of fever and dysentry two months later. After a gallantly successful assault against Panama on Christmas Day, he fell ill and died in January 1596.

Nevertheless, as disturbing as this news was to Elizabeth and her mariners, their highly-bouyant determination and pride were quick to recover. Brushing aside their overt sorrow, the Queen authorised another strike at Spain; this time on the mainland, at Cadiz again.

Spain had always maintained that the humiliating defeat of the Armada in 1588 had been primarily the result of poor sailing conditions and inclement weather—a sentiment not entirely without some foundation—and rumours forever circulated England that another massive fleet was being assembled. Under the Earl of Essex, but coordinated by an Expeditionary Council, 150 boats left England—including 22 which were Dutch. Within three weeks they had reached Cadiz and the town was captured six hours later. Essex, as Commander of the Land Forces, took the majority of the soldiers ashore at Punta Camaron and soon secured San Lucar de Barrameda. He then urged the Council to approve his advance into the interior of Andalucia, claiming that having now secured the mouth of the Guadalquivir River they thereby controlled all access to Seville and Cordoba. But he was outvoted.

Within ten weeks the fleet was back home again, the Queen full of praise for the military aspects of the trip but alarmed at the meagre quantities of bullion which they had brought back for her treasury. But now it was the Earl of Essex' time to enjoy the acclaim of his countrymen and Lord Howard was inspired to write to Lord Hunsdon that "there is not a braver man in the world than the Earl . . ." Their mercenary monarch, however, dropped him from her favours.

George Somers had not made the trip to Cadiz that year, but was invited by Essex to join him when he sailed to Spain the following year. In June 1597, the enthusiastic Earl of Essex—probably in order to vindicate himself in the eyes of his beloved Elizabeth—pulled anchor once more. His fleet had a variety of boats and certainly enjoyed the distinguished company of Sir Walter Raleigh and Lord Howard, as well as George Somers.

As usual, their specific target was the inevitable Armada which Queen Elizabeth had been repeatedly assured was still being assembled by the Spanish King, somewhere. It is not too unkind to say that after 40 demanding and gruelling years on the throne, the Queen was beginning to show signs of age and fatigue; she had begun to suspect that regular attempts were afoot to kill her (some were) and the irrepressible Spanish foe made her especially sensitive to any speculation that they might be about to peer from behind the Scilly Isles, at the mouth of the English Channel.

The fleet grouped at Plymouth and then headed into the ocean. But on the edge of the Bay of Biscay they encountered very high seas and turbulent weather. The boats were battered and separated; they were swamped with water, sails were ripped. Sailors were tossed overboard and drowned. Ironically, the Spaniards had decided not to proceed against England on account of this same stormy weather; but Essex, Somers and Raleigh were discovering this far too late. Unable to wrestle the disastrous conditions any further, word was conveyed to all ships that they should independently head for England. The expedition was scrubbed after four days of fighting nothing but storms!

In absolute despair, desperate to restore his tarnished image in the eyes of the Queen, Essex did not turn for home; instead he made for The Azores. As he had the previous year, the Earl was accompanied by the poet John Donne. The recently-encountered storm became the subject of his poems: "The Calm" and "The Storm."

Another literary remark. Had the fleet not been embarrassed by the weather, Essex intended sailing straight for Cadiz once more; this time the defiant and single-minded Earl planned to penetrate into the interior of Andalucia and capture Seville—which is what he wanted to do the previous year. It is an anecdoctal footnote for the History of Literature to record that he didn't do that. If he had attacked Seville that year then he would surely have disrupted the tranquil atmosphere of the Seville prison and prevented completion of a famous book. At that precise moment, a writer named Miguel de Cervantes was sitting in a cell penning the first chapters of a story which he later published as "Don Quixote."

By the time that the entire weather-beaten fleet had eventually struggled back into various English ports, it was quickly realised that George Somers and his ship were missing. Not for the first time in his life, he was reported missing and presumed to have been lost at sea. However, George Somers had already cultivated the habits of initiative and resourcefulness and no-one seriously gave him up for dead—least of all Joane Somers and the people of Lyme Regis.

In affirmation of their confidence, one dull morning in October, a small fishing boat watched a far larger galleon enter Lyme harbour; it tied against The Cobb. George Somers was back. Amidst much local excitement and relief he somewhat casually told how at the height of the storm he had chosen to save his boat and crew, by taking refuge in a small bay on the coast of France. There, they had spent the time repairing damage and preparing to make themselves seaworthy once again. It was a decision which had obviously saved their lives. From France they had touched briefly in Plymouth before leaving for home and only then had they learnt the details of what had happened to the remainder of the original fleet.

In 1598-9, Queen Elizabeth made moves to increase her navy by a further sixteen ships, whilst increasing her regular standing armed forces to six thousand men. It was partly in response to defence requirements, but also a private reaction to continued sensitivity about her personal safety. She had become hyper-sensitive to even the most glib and unfavourable comments; she felt the threat of assassination to be lurking everywhere. Shadows and sudden movements caused her to jerk, she became fertive. Her circle of trusted advisors narrowed.

On August 4th. 1598 her closest advisor died. He was Lord Burleigh. His son Sir Robert Cecil assumed his positions and power. The Cecils and Essex had always been at odds with each other and the ability of the Earl of Essex to retain any favour at all with the Queen was seen as a remarkable personal triumph— albeit a triumph of the heart rather than political influence.

In 1600, George Somers joined another Royal fleet. He had now established total credibility as a seaman and navigator; his sense of direction was recognised as being unusually sharp. Financial backers seemed convinced that he could never get lost, could find anywhere; would never return empty-handed. Priva-teering offered them all great rewards and few were those who cared to rebuff such enticing opportunities. That summer, as Captain of "Vanguard," he spent most of his time loitering about The Azores; slipping around headlands and lying in secluded bays; sitting, waiting for Spanish galleons and merchantmen to return from the West Indies and Africa.

For ten weeks, he successfully dodged the well-armed fleets of Spain, who waited to escort the returning ships on the last stage of their journey home. By September, he was stretched leisurely before the great fireplace in the parlour at Berne Manor, his wife by his side and more riches to decorate their house.

Whilst George Somers had decided to head south that summer of 1600, the partnership of Essex and Henry Wriothesley, the

Earl of Southampton, had made for Ireland. Still straining for complete acceptance back into the innermost of Royal Chambers, they were fighting in a campaign which, even by 1600, had already been ominously branded as "The Irish Question." It was their last joint venture. Essex had less than one year left to live.

On 19th. February 1601, Robert Devereaux, the 2nd. Earl of Essex, was found guilty of treason and sentenced to death. There is no doubt that he had planned a coup d'etat, scheming with Wriothesley to capture strategic buildings in London and overthrow the government; but he maintained that it was the only way he had of getting the Queen to sit down and talk to him! Six days later, he was beheaded. His partner, the Earl of Southampton, was reprieved and placed in cold storage, in The Tower.

Within a few months of these amazing events, George Somers was once again drawn into battle. This time he was aboard "Swiftsure," on a State mission to Ireland. On the basis of totally reliable sources, it had been learnt that Spain intended to send a mighty Armada to attack Ireland and then toss its hearty support behind an Irish rebellion. Somers was part of the naval task force sent to repel such a move.

This time, the Queen's nemesis had indeed proved true to his word. The Spanish attacked the coast of Ireland with over 5,000 men, all under the command of D'Aguilar, a considerably well-respected warrior who had long been the thorn in the side of English shipping. With military precision, D'Aguilar landed his troops at Kinsale, a spot southwards from Cork and on a part of the heavily indented coastline of Ireland where any navigation was notoriously hazzardous.

The subsequent fighting was vicious and bloody. On land, the men engaged in bitter combat; without mercy they hacked each other to death and slit the throats of the injured. Limbs were severed, and faces and bodies were blasted into ghastly forms by explosions and gunshot. At sea, "Swiftsure" zigzagged among the ships of Spain, her decks alive with a scurrying, sweaty crew which struggled hard to keep abreast of her ever-changing course. Somers glided skillfully and swerved his ship around the water, avoiding serious damage. And when the fighting was over and the Spaniards fell into retreat, George Somers was assigned the task of escorting the invaders southwards, making sure that they withdrew with dignity to Coruna.

By autumn, he was again back home in Dorset answering questions about his latest escapade. He could also give a full account of his meeting with Lord Mountjoy, the man who had actually been in charge of the entire battle. He had known

Charles Blount, Lord Mountjoy, for many years. He was a pleasantly plump military commander and had been appointed to serve as Lord Lieutenant for the attacks anticipated for that storm-defeated fleet of 1597. Cleared of any subsequent involvement with Essex and Southampton whilst they had all been serving together in Ireland, he was eventually made Earl of Devonshire and the owner of Kingston Hall—close to Upwey, in Dorset. Often these chance encounters in the field of battle were the only way which families heard of their loved-ones from faraway.

(Perhaps in belated homage to "Swiftsure" and George Somers, the name of the boat reappears in Naval Annals nearly three centuries later. In the 19th. century a three-masted clipper of 1,326 tons was given the same name.)

The following year, in 1602, George Somers headed back into the warmer waters where he was more comfortable. As captain of "Warspite" he toured the ravaged coasts of The Azores, as a member of a Royal fleet under the command of Captain Richard Leveson. As usual, their prime targets were the boats of Spain; their sole object being to capture prizes and return with more gold and silver for the English Treasury. "Warspite" had formerly sailed under Sir Walter Raleigh—a fact which George Somers was certainly very mindful about as he stood on the decks that particular year. Although little could he have guessed that within twelve months his friend would be dramatically toppled from favour, into The Tower.

Other than these voyages, there has also been much speculation that prior to 1609, George Somers made several more journeys to the West Indies. Outstanding Bermudian historian, Henry C. Wilkinson, suggests that these were probably at about this particular time, but they cannot be sufficiently corroborated.

Referring to the period 1585 to 1607, a prominent historian at the United States Department of the Interior states: "it is close to impossible to come up with even a partial list of ships names and Captains." His opinion goes on to add that during this time there were numerous English ships involved in raids against the Spanish West Indies—many of whom may have touched upon the coast of North America on their way home. Other records indicate that there may have been as many as 40 ships sailing these waters each year, few of whom have been identified. The years 1600-1607 are particularily uncertain. In short, it is impossible to verify that George Somers really did visit this region as is so often stated; or, indeed whether he had ever been to North

America before 1610. All such speculation hinges on the casual remark of a shipmate who suggests that he had often been to North America; but there is no proof at all.

A voyage made in 1603 has sometimes been cited as an occasion when he may have visited the area around Virginia, but this is also not supported by facts. In 1603, Bartholomew Gilbert sailed to Virginia in "Elizabeth," probably continuing the desperate quest to locate any signs of Raleigh's first colonists, who had settled the Chesapeake Bay and Roanoke Island vicinity. Gilbert, however, was killed by Indians and his boat returned with eleven survivors under the expert care of the boat's mate, Henry Sute. There is absolutely no reference in the official report of George Somers being with them.

The foremost scholar for this particular period, David Beers Quinn, notes that there is only a very fine web of speculation about English activities on the coast northwards of the Spanish zone, between 1600 and 1605. Quinn claims that the 1602 voyage made by Captain Samuel Mace was the fifth which Raleigh had organised to try and find his colonists. He proposes that two others may have taken place in 1600 and 1601. Arguably, therefore, if George Somers had ever visited North America before, then he may have done it on either of these occasions. But again there is no proof whatsoever; and from the activities which we can establish for him during those years, it is highly improbable that he did head West.

In the words of one United States Government official: ". . . although others may have sailed to Virginia during this period, there is no definite knowledge of their activities... Somers has not been linked with any of these voyages to Virginia."

Immediately after his successful privateering trip to The Azores in 1602, George Somers began to devote his energies towards planning the construction of a ship which he would call "Sea Venture." At the same time, he started to help in the funding and organising of projects which would ultimately lead him to Virginia and Bermuda in 1609.

11

Into A New Phase

By 1601, it had become abundantly clear that the excitement and effervescence which had once typified the Elizabethan Age was rapidly on the wane. It was public knowledge that the Queen herself was deteriorating both physically and mentally, that 40 years of wearing the crown had taken its toll.

She had grown weary of the incessant fighting which proved so essential to increasing the country's wealth. She was frustrated that the more peaceable policy of colonisation had made little progress. Above all she was perpetually disturbed by the threats of assassination which she suspected of abounding everywhere; she had developed an overwhelming persecution complex which bordered on paranoia—a state which had not been relieved by the formation of the grandly titled "Association for the Defence of the Life of Queen Elizabeth," created in 1585.

Her earlier years had been shaped by glamour and promise; they were the days of flamboyant courtiers , debonair seamen and endless lines of handsome suitors. They had been times of colour, gaiety and hope. But the once radiant, trend-setting monarch entered the seventeenth century as a manic-depressive; a recluse unrecognisable from her former self. When her godson Sir John Harrington visited her in October of 1601, he was shattered by her appearance. He told a friend that her features had altered drastically and her form had become skeletal; she was, he reported, eating nothing but "bread and pottage, she had not changed her clothes for many days; she was the torment of the ladies who waited on her." Her conduct was evidently peculiar too; Harrington notes that she stamped her feet and was randomly violent with those who perchanced nearby. It had become normal for her to sit with a sword at her side and she frequently slashed at the tapestries by the dining-table, expecting to strike the murderers she felt were always nearby.

By 1602, Sir John declared that "she was in a more piteable state"—which was difficult to imagine! It had become hard to reconcile this image with the sensuous young monarch who had once proudly boasted of a wardrobe with 300 gowns and 30 wigs, but this was the tragic spectacle which they had to accept. (Harrington was rumoured to have been the illegitimate son of William Shakespeare, the outcome of a hasty daliance which he purportedly had with a lady from the bar of a London tavern; although what qualification this had for him to become a godson of the Queen is unclear.)

This ugly deterioration was steadily monitored by William Gilbert, the Royal Physician; retained for the annual stipend of one hundred pounds, he loyally stayed with her throughout and became privy to her inner-most concerns when she lapsed into spells of deleriousness. On one such occasion she revealed that her life had always been privately tormented by persistent gossip that her mother, Ann Boleyn, had been a partial freak with an extra finger on one hand and the bizarre signs of a third breast!

At 3 a.m. on 24th. March 1603, Elizabeth died. It was the Eve of the Annunciation. Physician Gilbert was with her to the last gasp—and was destined to follow her along that same path to glory just eight months later.

In some respects, the grief-stricken Nation was mourning the end of the Elizabethan Age, rather than the loss of the weak, demented woman who had been its inspiration. But although her death was indeed an historic milestone which saddened every-one, there was healthy consolation to be taken from the events of her last few years. Ironically she had been incapable of grasping at the landmarks which now promised great hope for the immediate future; those perceptions she had left to her advisors.

Voyages like those which George Somers had made between 1600-2 demonstrated that her seamen were controlling the seas as never before; successes like those which he made to The Azores, Spain, Ireland and Portugal proved that England could adequately defend herself against any threats. Elizabeth had bequeathed a fresh confidence, a determination unique in their traditional history of seafaring. Even her visions for colonisation were germinating and as recently as 1602 Bartholomew Gosnold had paved the way for that final thrust which would result in permanent settlements in North America. There was even symbolic good fortune to be gleaned from the return of Sir Richard Hawkins, recently ransomed after many years of imprisonment by the Spaniards. And the future of the Empire looked bright—in 1600 Elizabeth had authorised a Charter for a group of London traders to expand into India, an act which ultimately resulted in the formation of the East India Company.

The picture was far less gloomy than she suspected. It was true that The Age had lost many of its heroic sailors—Drake, Hawkins, Frobisher, Grenville and the Gilbert brothers had all died. But England was still blessed with mariners of the calibre of Walter Raleigh, John Davis, James Lancaster, George Somers and Christopher Newport; men on whom the country could rely with great confidence.

And there was comfort too from Elizabeth's legacy in the realm of European Affairs. Since 1598, when Philip III ascended the throne of Spain, a permanent peaceful settlement had consistently edged closer to final reality. He was perhaps universally despicted as wanton, languid and indolent; an inept person whose incompetence had been epitomised by his reckless expulsion of all Muslems from Spain—an act which in one single sweep had robbed Spain of her leading merchants, artists and financiers! Extravagantly he spent freely on events of Court—bullfights, fiestas and banquets—spending at a rate far greater than his abused galleons could possibly manage to meet. Peace had thus become an obvious solution to his diminishing coffers because it would instantly reduce his defence budget!

Elsewhere in Europe, the Hapsburgs had created the independent state of Belgium, tactfully ruled by Archduke Albert (Maximillian's son) and his wife Isabella (Philip of Spain's daughter). That area was now enjoying considerable success as a centre for arts and commerce. And in Austria and Germany, efforts were afoot to centralise the fragmented states into one Empire—a task which the Hapsburgs could only manage to accomplish providing that their unbalanced ruler Rudolph II (1576-1612) continued to voluntarily lock himself away in one of his castles in Prague!

The end of the Elizabethan Age was therefore not one of gloom, but one of promise. The diverse events of the Queen's reign had collectively created the springboard from which the seventeenth century would be able to leap ahead.

* * * * * *

In Dorset, life was flourishing and prosperous. Many felt that the quayside had never been so filled with boats, nor The Cobb so busy. The market stalls were always stacked with the usual variety of goods and the people of Lyme Regis seemed happy and content. The blossoming prosperity manifested itself in the total renovation of "The Shambles" market at the bottom of Broad Street—a project to which George Somers had made generous contributions; and it revealed itself in smaller ways, such as the fine plasterwork which was being completed in 1601 on the frontage of "Tudor House," near St. Michael's Church. For an exorbitant and tempting sum, the Williams family had sold Colway Manor to a new owner, Robert Henley of Winsham.

Likewise, George Somers continued to prosper with it. He had social standing and respect; was a man of comfortable means, in part due to his activities as a privateer.

In 1598, he had finally managed to save enough money to be able to buy the full quitclaim deeds to Upwey Manor, a transaction which he and Joane completed with Raynold Keate of Chiselborne. On August 30th. of that same year he had also been made a Freeman of Lyme like his father before him and this now offered him unprecedented chances of commercial opportunities, rights and privileges. He could have first options on goods directly at The Cobb; could have things set aside for later, or for trading with "foreign" customers. These were traders not only from Holland or Germany, but also those from Honiton and Axminster. They were all foreigners, outsiders. There were also limited tax concessions for the Freemen and priority treatment for having goods released by the customs officials. The rewards were great and the penalties for abuse were severe.

By pure coincidence, the year that George Somers was being made a Freeman of Lyme, Silvester Jourdain was being deprived of the same honour. Friends since childhood, Jourdain had matured into a less-than-noble adult. In 1597 he had appeared in the Lyme Court for having urinated in the garden of the resident Latin teacher; such was the crudeness of the man! Then in 1598 he had been rather vaguely charged with being "contumacious" as a Freeman and ordered to stay behind in the Town Hall at the conclusion of the day's business, so that he could contemplate alone on his foolishness. The punishment was a detention called "a breeze." However, as soon as the last councillor left so Silvester Jourdain strutted out defiantly behind him. The subsequent forfeiture of his Freemanship was a serious economic blow for the family and another dent in his dubious reputation.

But the fate of Silvester Jourdain was of no consequence to the Somers clan. George Somers was still a rising star and respect continued to mount for him and his family. Even the court appearance of a wayward Somers, probably nephew Matthew, in 1596, "for brawling and drawing blood" had been forgotten upon payment of a fine.

In the peaceful seclusion of Berne Manor, George and Joane could enjoy the generous tranquility lavished upon them by life in the country. They socialised with the William Floyer family, rich landowners from Whitchurch Canonicorum, and visited the new owners of Colway Manor. They attended St. Wita's Church regularily, prayed, listened to the sermons and in 1602 probably even congratulated Mr. and Mrs. Lacombe on the birth of their baby son. (None of them knew, of course, that he would become Lyme's most disreputable preacher! A man of the cloth whose reputation as a controversial orator of lecherous moral fibre would follow him to America later in life!)

In 1603, sitting in their usual pew in church, listening to the pleasant sounds of the brand new bells which had just been installed, George Somers must have been a contented man indeed. He had been good to life and it, in turn, was now repaying the compliment. There were obvious rewards.

Joane Somers was hardly the wealthiest wife in Dorset, but then her wardrobe was not the leanest either. With taffeta, silk and linens so readily available from her husband's privateering ventures, her closets boasted many gowns made from these fine materials. For extra special occasions she favoured a long dress, emphasised at the hips by a full, padded roll which elegantly threw the material outwards in a descending flair. Ruffs were forever popular, daintily rising on a wired support from the shoulders up high to the crown of the hairstyle. To display her jewellery, Joane also favoured clothes with an open front, a fashion which left the chest bare above the breast-line—an ideal space for showing-off necklaces and pendants. And she doubtless had a fine selection of folding fans to chose from, to help her to strike that impressive pose for those who might watch her arriving at functions in Lyme Regis. How splendid she must have been, clad in rich silks or followed by the swish of taffeta!

George Somers, of course, was a man of taste. His clothing also favoured silks and satins cut into the most fashionable styles. In 1602 men wore neck-ruffs and sported padded jackets fastened at the front by a row of neatly descending ball-buttons. They liked to strut in trunk-hose, puffed shorts with slashed panels inset into them so as to reveal a fabric of contrasting colour to the rest of the costume. He wore stockings fastened at the knee and often a long loose robe slipped over his shoulders for evening wear. As he rode into Lyme astride his favourite horse, who could have failed to notice such a fine, proud, seafaring peacock?

But there was a price to be paid for such fame and fortune, a price which made continuous demands on his time. He was regarded as an authority on Atlantic shipping and commerce, was reknowned as a navigator, and his association with Raleigh and the Gilberts had made his opinions and ideas about colonialism much sought-after; especially by investors and trading companies. He was an ideal intermediary between those who financed voyages and those who actually made them; his was a unique and valuable perspective of intentions versus limitations; between what was ideal and what was practical.

Such commitments frequently took him to London, a city were he had become quite relaxed and at home. For Joane it meant more time left on her own at Berne Manor, although this had always been the nature of their entire married life; at least she may have felt some consolation in his being probably safer in London than he was out somewhere at sea.

Just as George Somers' life was entering a new phase, then so was England as whole starting anew. As soon as Elizabeth uttered her last gasps, there was immediate consent to invite James VI of Scotland to take over as King of England.

It was an ironic choice, in that his mother was the Mary Queen of Scots whom Elizabeth had had beheaded two decades earlier. On the other hand, it was a wise choice which diplomatically aimed at reconciling the two Kingdoms. It won widespread approval, at first. James, however, was not among the strongest of persons and his odd upbringing had made him awkward and uncomfortable with strangers. He was clearly very well educated but had never been a philosopher, a weakness which didn't help to impregnate his reign with ideas and plans. Furthermore, his peculiar family life had led him to be even more paranoid about assassinations than Elizabeth had been—and he was doubtless the first English monarch ever to wear a sword-proof vest to breakfast. As an infant, he experienced the gory death of his father, Henry Stewart—killed by an explosion which many believed to be authorised by Mary herself. Then he had to watch his loving mother being pursued and persecuted by Sir Francis Walsingham for many years, before then being beheaded. Such exceptional events must have had some significance in moulding the eccentric behaviour of the new King. He hated the sight of drawn swords and was ill-at-ease with unfamiliar people, places and things. But, for all his weaknesses, England showed a willingness to ignore his peculiar accent and strange traits.

Once in London, he set about securing personal support from those whose help he would need once installed. He held meetings, interviews and debates and tried to curry favour with the rich, wise and powerful by distributing new ranks and titles upon their shoulders. During 1603, the first year of his reign, he managed to bestow no fewer than 1,053 knighthoods on citizens across the land.

Many of these new Knights already held the title and found themselves honoured with another version. Others were given the Royal Blessing by virtue of their influence in one town or another which James deemed to be of value in attracting widespread personal approval. In the months preceding his coronation, he undertook a tour of the Kingdom—a nostalgic homage to the popular "progresses" for which Elizabeth had been so loved. It gave him a chance to see his inherited country, whilst giving his subjects the chance to see what he looked like in the flesh.

In some ways, this Regal Tour bore a close resemblance to a travelling theatre, the Royal entourage excitedly flustering around its new leading actor. It was an extraordinary tour of mutual acquaintance, one which aimed at gathering into the majestic flock as many people as possible, as quickly as possible.

On 13th. April, they were in Newcastle with a knighthood for Nicholas Tufton and other local dignitaries; then on to York where the exalted Lord Burghley was curiously awarded the lesser title of Knight Bachelor. From here the caravan went to Durham with an impressive be-knighting ceremony in Belvoir Castle. Next they wove victoriously westwards to knight Thomas Preston of Dorset and his neighbours, and then into Somerset to catch William Dyer and John Carew. Then it was back to Devon to make Edward Seymore a Knight. Gradually turning their way back to London, James and his party stopped near Salisbury to grant a knighthood to William Herbert; Thomas Preston must also have got in the way for records show that he received his second knighthood in two months, on that same day! Also present was Henry Wriothesley—recently released from The Tower by the new King-designate. (Pardoning a man who had tried to overthrow the previous ruler, one might have thought, was brazen enough—but to then confer a knighthood on him was surely taking it too far!)

As soon as his coronation was fixed for July 25th., James seems to have become more eager than ever to award further honours. On July 17th. 1603, he issued a general summons to all gentlemen who owned land valued at 40 pounds or more, directing them to travel to London to receive the honour of Knight Bachelor, the lowest of the Orders. On 23rd. July, some 461 men had responded—"nearly all"—and they dutifully assembled in the Royal Garden at Whitehall for their official investiture at the hands of the King in person. Among the group were Francis Bacon of Hertfordshire; Thomas May of Sussex; Thomas Gresham of Titsey in Surrey; and George Somers of Dorset.

The recipients were gathered into smaller more manageable batches and James formally conferred the titles of each of them; it was a beautiful day, warm and sunny, and the manicured gardens made it a perfect setting for such a noble occasion. In the crowd, George Somers noticed the neighbourly face of Thomas Freake of Sherbourne Manor; he also recognised Robert Prideaux of Devon and Robert Brown of Dorset. Each became a Knight Bachelor.

After the somewhat brief ceremonies were over, most of the new knights remained in London for the coronation of King James I. Even that occasion was not to be missed as a chance to grant more honours. Once crowned, James conferred the elitist rank of "Knight of the Bath" on a select handful of men, in fair recognition of various services which they had rendered to the country. These included Philip Herbert, Robert Carr (the Earl of Somerset), Robert Rich (the Earl of Warwick); William Herbert—his second knighthood in three weeks!—and Christopher Hatton of Northamptonshire.

In early August, Sir George and Lady Somers made their first formal appearance in Lyme Regis and received the heartfelt congratulations of their kinsfolk. Meanwhile, at Berne, the domestic staff eagerly awaited the return of their "new" Master and Mistress. At Whitchurch Canonicorum, the congregation of St. Wita's would have to wait until the following Sunday before they could share in the widespread excitement of greeting such distinguished worshippers.

By the end of 1603, Sir George Somers had gently become more and more ensnared in a pact with fate. He was holding detailed discussions with Richard Hakluyt, Edward Wingfield, John Smith, Bartholomew Gosnold and Sir Thomas Gates concerning the possibilities of future voyages to North America. In November, Walter Raleigh was sentenced to death for treason; he was reprieved on 15th. December but would spend the next twelve years in The Tower. The future hopes for colonisation now rested in the hands of this nucleus of men.

In the small town of Alpenburgh on the coast of Suffolk, a handful of shipwrights had started to construct a new sailing ship which would eventually be known as "Sea Venture."

THE ARMS OF THE LONDON VIRGINIA COMPANY

12

A Public Servant

Even though he had always been very active in community affairs, 1604 was something of a peak in Sir George Somers' career as a public servant. During that single year he was elected Mayor of Lyme Regis and was then simultaneously appointed to serve as the town's Member of Parliament, in London. Individually each was an onerous position, but together they made demands which taxed even Sir George's proven organisational skills.

The Mayor's term ran for twelve months, from September to September. He had been involved with the Town Council for many years and had participated in numerous debates and discussions on the development of Lyme; following his elevation to Freeman in 1598, it was incumbent upon him to serve on various local committees and it was from this pool of Freemen that "Burgesses" were chosen—the men who would serve as Town Councillors.

The Town Council consisted of fifteen or so members. It was realised that not all of them could always attend each meeting, but with fifteen committeemen it was assumed that there would always be a quorum to attend to the daily business of Lyme Regis. It met on a weekly basis and dealt with topics ranging from taxes, fines and levies, through to trading disputes and sewage disposal. All decisions were carefully recorded and if there happened to be an item of regional significance, then the Recorder was expected to re-write another copy and place it on file among the County Records in Dorchester.

George Somers' name features quite consistently over a lengthy period of time in these minutes suggesting that, contrary to popular belief, his elevation to the lofty position of Mayor was not a casual reward for a man of local prestige—but was the natural promotion of a townsman who had expended considerable time and energy on the well-being of his birth-place.

Whilst Sir George served as Mayor, the official Recorder for the Council was John FitzJames, a fellow-burgess with a particular flair for words. His records are detailed yet precise and carefully written in that modified copper-plate scrawl so characteristic of the period, with flowing lines, waves and whisps decorating each page. At the bottom, he dutifully entered the names of those Councillors who were present at each session. Since Lyme also enjoyed the right to conduct its own minor court, the position of Mayor brought with it the added obligation of serving as the resident Justice of the Peace. Memoranda of verdicts were also placed on file.

Among these flakey documents we can find descriptions of minor disputes, cases of theft and instances of dubious trading practices; but there were also more serious issues covered by The Council. One document dated 27th. August 1604 involves their effort to establish a legal precedent, an interpretation of the respective powers of the Burgesses themselves as envisaged in the original Charter. Another dated October 1st. deals with the incorrect suspension of Robert Hazzard, one of the Councillors, whose position had been withdrawn because he was then being cited in a case pending before the High Court of the Star Chamber. This was seen as the highest court in the land, the one to which the commoners felt that they had free access to bring charges against local dignitaries and land-barons. (Actually, James II disbanded this traditional right in 1641.)

Why it was that "one John Roze of our town" had decided to take Councillor Hazzard before that august body was not on record in Lyme; their concern was only to restore his rights until such a time as he might be found guilty. The Council kindly vowed to await the outcome verdict of the Crown Mediator, Lord Windon.

Frequently, Mayor Somers and his Council arbitrated in minor disputes. There is, for example, the story of John Wilsdon who was summonsed to explain why he had sold a barrel of foreign wine to a vintner named Berry, without the proper licence. He was fined and the wine was confiscated. Similarly, John Lumbry of Charmouth was given a hefty fine for selling a barrel of figs at well over the current rate. And in January 1605 Robert Hardie offered no defence to the charge that he had overpriced a keg of Gascony wine; he too was fined.

Whenever Sir George was away on business, Deputy Mayor Richard Norris took his place. It was his misfortune to be Acting-Mayor when the Council handled the curious matter of two sheep skins which had been stolen and then abandoned in the town centre; after due time, they had been auctioned off . . . now William Legg was claiming compensation as the original owner!

But if this was the nature of things on the Lyme Regis Council, then it was all quite different for the Members of Parliament in London. As the M.P. for Lyme Regis, Sir George was a priviledged party to some of the major decisions of his day. 1604 was the year when The Treaty of London was signed between England and Spain, the conclusion to over one hundred years of warfare between the two Nations. He was also in the House of Commons in June that year when a censure motion was debated and passed against Sir Henry Wriothesley on charges that he had been "improperly intimate with the Queen"—a verbal discourtesy, the members were assured! And he sat on the oak back-benches in December and solemnly listened to the news that Captain John Davis had been killed by Japanese pirates off the coast of Sumatra, where he had been on a mission with Sir Edward Michelbourne on behalf of the East Indies Company.

On a personal level, 1604 also marked the sad death of his father-in-law—in fact he had had to rush back from London to arrange for the small family funeral and comfort Joane. Philip Heywood had always been a kindly man and he and Sir George had shared in a most cordial relationship. He was not particularily wealthy, but he was jovial and generous of spirit.

Sir George and Lady Somers were back in London at the end of the year as guests at the much-publicised marriage of Sir Philip Herbert. He was the unpredictable, gallant, silly, mean, reckless and utterly charming brother of Sir William Herbert. In December he married Susan, the daughter of Edward de Vere, the 17th. Earl of Oxford. It was the social event of the year, most extravagant in size and magnificance. Gifts amounted to thousands of pounds, including a land-grant from King James reputedly worth 500 pounds annual rent.

George Somers knew the Herbert family through Sir Walter Raleigh and had often visited them at Wilton Hall, on the outskirts of Salisbury. Their father was the 4th. Earl of Pembroke; their mother was Mary—probably the most erudite and literary person in royal circles; a lady said to have been far more interested in translating French prose than she was in the affairs of State. Friendship with this family enabled Sir George to overlap into the social circles of the Nation's most eminent financiers, aristocrats and the leading characters of English literature.

As an M.P., he was involved with decisions on domestic issues, as well as being exposed to far-reaching topics of foreign and economic affairs. It was in London that he learnt to understand the implications behind the rise of Pope Paul V; it was in the House that he grasped the significance of the founding of Tomsk in Siberia—and the connection between the death of Boris Godunoff and the fate of the Muscovy Trading Company. He listened to the reports of sub-committees who followed the gradual decline of the Indian Mogul Jehan Jir, from grand schemes to rule the whole world into a life of alcohol and opium. He read papers about the capture of Tabriz by Shah Abbas of Persia; he followed the debate which focused on the effects which the newly proclaimed Shogun Iyeyasu would have on trade with Japan and the use of the port to Tokyo.

He was being exposed to the world in a way which was exclusive to national government. Since becoming an M.P. on 25th. February 1604 he was firmly established at the heart of the country; his name and face were familiar to the most important persons in England. He knew and was known by many. He was intimate with political moods, watched the subtle switches which occurred to its pulse. He wandered easily in the midst of poets, bankers, merchants, Dukes, warriors, seamen, and potential investors.

The list of his friends and acquaintances had grown longer and longer. As a political figure on the London scene he knew members of the families of the Earls of Southampton, Warwick, Pembroke and Somerset; he knew the Treasurer of England, Sir Thomas Sackville, and King James' leading advisor, Sir Robert Cecil, the Lord Salisbury. And whenever he chose to saunter into the Mermaid Tavern on Bread Street—one of the most frequented ale houses in London—he was peripherally involved with The Friday Street Club founded by his old friend Sir Walter Raleigh. Over a drink with political colleagues, he could listen to the conversations, readings and wit-combat between members of the foremost literary circle of the period. Here he became familiar with Ben Jonson, John Donne, Samuel Daniel, William Camden, Francis Bacon, Fulke Grenville, and William Shakespeare. (It was this casual relationship between Shakespeare and Somers which would subsequently be the prime motive behind Shakespeare's writing "The Tempest.")

Bread Street, just off Cheapside in the centre of London, was "lined with divers inns." It was the place where England's most influential figures went to relax, drink, talk confidentially. Why Raleigh had opted to popularise The Mermaid Tavern we do not know. But he did, and it became the focal point for London life in the first decade of the seventeenth century. George Somers was one of the group. There is no reason to believe that he was drawn into the drunkeness and debauchery which attracted so many of the others, but he most certainly went there often. He heard Ben Jonson toasting the absent, imprisoned Sir Walter Raleigh and listened to him repeating his recollection of the time when they both got drunk together, in Paris. And whenever the ridiculous Sir Philip Herbert happened to be present there was never any lacking of baudy stories and drunken outbursts of verbal and physical violence.

In the autumn of 1605, Sir George found himself almost fatally too close to one of the darker pages in English history. After the summer recess, James had originally decreed that the new session of Parliament would open on 3rd. October, but then in late September he delayed the convening for another month—until November 5th. It was a move which came frighteningly close to altering the face of England . . . one which almost deprived Lyme of its Mayor, and Bermuda of its Founder.

In retrospect, the attempted coup led by the Earl of Essex in 1601 was no mere isolated case. It was an indicator of national unrest which should have been taken more seriously. Specifically, attention should have been paid to the sizeable Catholic community in England—estimated to have been about one third of the population.

In May of 1603, Sir William Catesby, an ardent Catholic who had been wounded and imprisoned for his role in the Earl of Essex plot, developed his own plan to assassinate the King. Even though James had hardly had chance to warm the throne, Catesby felt that he had no sympathy for Catholics. He recruited his cousin John Winter into the scheme and by the summer of 1605 had increased it to include: Thomas Percy, John and Christopher Wright, Francis Tresham, Sir Everard Digby and Ambrose Rockwood. Each of them became a conspirator in what has since become known as "The Gunpowder Plot." Lacking a man with proven military talents and bravery, Thomas Winter was sent off to Holland to recruit the services of Guy Fawkes—a Yorkshireman who had been serving in the Spanish Army since 1598.

When King James delayed the Opening of Parliament, he

thereby gave Catesby and his followers more time to solidify their plans. They rented a cellar beneath the House of Lords and Fawkes was able to hide in it twenty barrels of gunpowder, which he covered with piles of harmless wood and similarly innocuous bits of debris.

By October, the King had announced that his very popular son Prince Henry would also attend the proceedings. This must have filled the plotters with glee. They were already assured that each Member of Parliament would be there by Royal Summons, as well as many of the more prominent clergymen of the Church of England. Catesby now realised that he would have the entire hierarchy of the country sitting directly above his rented cellar on November 5th.

Like the rest of his colleagues, Sir George Somers had already reached London the week before the start of the new session. He had left Lyme Regis in the middle of October, allowing himself various one-night stopovers en route to visit friends, and had reached his offices in London with plenty of time to spare. This time was fruitfully spent on preparations for the upcoming parliamentary session—one which was expected to be hectic and eventful—although not for the reasons which Catesby had in mind.

Francis Tresham has been described as a "mean, treacherous and unprincipled character," but he evidently also had some weak and human spots for it was his kind consideration for others which led to the collapse of the plot—and hence spared the life of George Somers and everyone else. Tresham's two sisters had married the Lords Monteagle and Huston. Lord Monteagle was a known Catholic sympathiser who had also been involved with the Earl of Essex scheme of 1601, in fact he had been imprisoned for his part in that debaucle. (He had somehow managed to pay a fine of 8,000 pounds to buy his release, as well as the favour of James I.) Anyway, Tresham decided to send a letter to Monteagle, suggesting in no precise terms that the pair of them should really try to think of somewhere else to go on that particular day—anywhere, so long as it was well clear of the buildings! He wrote it on 26th. October. Sir George Somers was by then already in London, following his ride from Dorset.

Lord Monteagle had entered Parliament at the same time as Somers and they had served their first year in those chambers together. Upon receiving Tresham's letter, this about-faced Lord promptly showed it to Lord Salisbury, the most senior and trusted advisor of the King. Salisbury cautiously delayed passing the information on to his monarch until 3rd. November, for fear that somehow the plotters might get wind of it and make their escape. On the night of November 4th., Salisbury directed a rapid and sudden search which swept all adjacent grounds and buildings; there, comfortably nestled in the back of one cellar they uncovered the gunpowder, with Mr. Fawkes sitting nearby.

At what had literally been the fabled eleventh hour, the audacious Gunpowder Plot had been foiled. And on the 5th. November, on schedule, Sir George Somers took his seat thirty feet away from King James, settled comfortably into his allotted oaken pew and took part in the Opening of Parliament.

Naturally news of the attempted assassination was all over London on the morning after the capture of Guy Fawkes—and Sir George may well have pricked his ears upon learning that one of the conspirators was named Thomas Winter. Was it the same person that he knew from Dorset? But it wasn't; the majority of the plotters were from the Midlands. Whilst the confusion was still being sorted-out, James declared that the entire parliamentary session should be adjourned until January of the next year—just a few months away—which would allow the government an opportunity to thoroughly investigate the plot and uproot the causes. With that announcement, Sir George and his colleagues rose, bowed to the King and Prince Henry, and filed from the panelled chamber.

Over the next few days, Lord Salisbury directed the operations which resulted in the death or capture of all of those who had been implicated. Guy Fawkes had proved quite willing to reveal absolutely everything, with the inducement of some unsavoury tortures; in the dark, dank dungeons beneath London he speedily identified his friends and their probable whereabouts. Catesby, Percy and Wright had sped towards western England and Wales where they expected to be able to arouse the support of the large Catholic enclaves in these parts. By 8th. November they had got as far as Staffordshire. But there was no popular uprising, no sympathy; instead, they were killed by the Royalist regional forces. The remainder of the plotters were duly arrested and returned to London to stand trial. Probably as an expedient opportunity and excuse, Lord Salisbury also arrested the leader of the Puritan movement of England, a priest named Garnet, and somehow contrived to link him with the other plotters in the assassination attempt.

Sir George Somers emerged from these extraordinary events quite unscathed; he doned cape and cap and rode back to Berne Manor for Christmas; but wherever he went or showed his face he was constantly besieged by friends and neighbours who wanted to know exactly what had happened on that night in London when there had been a Gunpowder Plot. George was certainly in a position to offer them a first-hand description; and Joane was presumably relieved that he was still alive to sit and answer their questions.

On schedule, Parliament reconvened the following January, but conversation still centred upon the trial of Fawkes and the others. They all made appearances before a special commission, were found guilty on 27th. January and were duly executed on February 1st. 1606. The gory deaths of these schemers began with a hanging, followed by the bloody mutilation of their corpses. These were days when savagery and barbarism were the bedfellows of fashionable silks and cultured chatter; England was, afterall, a civilised country. Crowds flocked into the streets to witness the revolting spectacle of Guy Fawkes and his associates; people clapped and applauded as limbs were severed, stomachs were disembowelled and heads were held high aloft on spiked staves. Almost certainly, somewhere in the crowd lingered the M.P. from Lyme Regis, standing with his political allies; heaving a sigh of relief that the plot had failed.

Once all of this revengeful violence was over, the parliamentarians returned to their seats and continued to debate the items on their lengthy agenda. Firstly, they decided that henceforth November 5th. should be designated "Guy Fawkes Day," to be an occasion highlighted by firework displays and the symbolic burning of an effigy of a figure called a "guy." Next they began working on a priority item of deciding on a committee of senior members who would commence the preparation of a new version of The Bible—the one subsequently known as "The King James Version."

They also learnt that on the previous 20th. December Captain John Smith had set off with a party of 165 emigrants, aiming to continue with the colonisation of North America. They discussed the merit of such voyage and George Somers spoke repeatedly for their support. They discussed the voyages which Captain Christopher Newport was making to The Virginias and offered praise for the courage of these men and their womenfolk; they offered their thanks to the brave seamen who ferried the pioneers over the seas and complimented the work of Bartholomew Gosnold and Ferdinando Gorges, each of whom was also deeply committed to the realisation of the colonial policy.

Once they were outside the tense inner-workings of government, the members relaxed in the inns of Bread Street and, on this occasion, must have all sniggered at the gossipy climax to the scandal which had involved Lady Penelope Rich and Sir Charles Blount. After an affair which had spanned a lifetime, the two aristocrats had finally managed to get married on 26th. December 1605 when Lord Rich agreed to his wife's request for a divorce. Sir George Somers knew both of them very well. And so it was that this beautiful lady—who also happened to be the sister of Robert Devereaux, the late Earl of Essex—married the man of her lusty dreams. (She had actually already left her husband some time before, taking her five children in tow as she publicly screamed that none of them had been sired by Lord Rich in the first place! One of them was Robert Rich.) The couple were married in the small village church of Wanstead in Essex. Sadly, the strain proved to be beyond his emotional constitution for on 3rd. April, the poor Sir Charles quietly slipped beyond both her and life itself—and he died, the lingering target for gossip and disdain in the ale houses along Bread Street.

The closure of Parliament must have given rise to a sigh of relief from the over-worked members. For Sir George Somers it mercifully offered the most welcome opportunity to return to the far slower pace of life in Dorset. Once home, he watched the builders completing some final work on the end of The Cobb and he also went to his church at Whitchurch Canonicorum to see how the French carvers were coming along with their skillful work of decorating the wooden ends of the pews.

But he also discovered that there was a fresh, special impetus around Lyme, one which conveyed the anticipation that greater things were about to happen on the seas. The concept of colonisation had really started to invoke local interest. People talked about it in the street, about what it would be like, who could go. Everywhere, from Cornwall to Norfolk, they paid more attention to reports which filtered back; they paid heed to the activities of the larger trading companies and digested what was being said about those places far, far away. Psychologically, England had reached a crucial stage of maturity. Colonies were no longer ignored as foolish, fanciful dreams.

On May 14th. 1607, Jamestown was officially established in Virginia. It was news which was greeted by unprecedented general excitement, as English families experienced the genuine thrill of being alive to witness the dawn of a new era. In a society which had traditionally boasted of its fascination for The Arts, it had suddenly become quite unimportant that in nearby Europe Monteverdi had just announced his completion of a major opera entitled "Orfeo."

13

The Rise Of The Virginia Company

Colonisation, of course, was not a new idea recently conceived at the turn of the seventeenth century. By then it had already been ageing like a bottle of wine, but one which had been forgotten at the back of the cellar. It was taken to be of only secondary importance to England's other trading policies and the onset of rigor mortis had only been averted under the skill and interest of the few.

Spain had established her first colonies in Hispaniola in 1493, the year after Christopher Columbus first visited "The New World," and had continued to colonise an entire Empire. The Spaniards had started the slave trade in 1503 to help them clear forests and build their churches and towns; by 1538 Jimenez de Guesada had founded a major settlement called Bogota, in Nuevo Granada (now Colombia). Her convoys were a regular sight, ferrying farmers, traders, priests, civil servants and their families to new lives throughout the Caribbean, and Central and South America. In 1541 they landed the first negroes and women in Venezuela for the prime purpose of creating a permanent hybrid society. Colonisation, by occupation and inbreeding, had become the mainstay of Spanish foreign policy.

England's comparative disinterest in such ventures was perhaps a matter of having different priorities, although English mariners could hardly have been encouraged by the rewards which Balboa, de Almagro and Gonzalo Pizarro received for their efforts to open new frontiers: each had been executed! It all made trading in wine and figs at Marseilles seem much safer!

The country's objectives were basically ones of exploration and discovery, in the hope that eventually trading possibilities might benefit from newer markets. It seemed to be pointless to leave people behind on those distant shores.

Needless to say, England had sent probes to the lands on the other side of the Atlantic. Even the Somers boys had heard the story of Albert de Prado, "a foreign priest living in London" who had taken two fine English ships out to the Americas in 1527—never to be heard from again! And they knew too about the journey made at about the same time by "a London gentleman named Hore"—although his vivid descriptions of "merciless hardships faced by us" were sufficient to squash further interest for several decades.

As a colonial power, England hadn't taken any significant steps until 1578, when Sir Humphrey Gilbert received royal assent to establish outposts closer to the West Indies from which he could attack the Spaniards more easily. On June 11th. 1583, he claimed Newfoundland for "Her Majesties pleasure" and planted his flag amidst great pomp and fanfare—witnessed by his half-brother Walter Raleigh. The excitement of this important occasion, however, was short-lived. On the way home, they fell afoul of a tempestuous storm—and the last that anyone ever saw of the gallant Sir Humphrey, he was reputedly sitting on the deck of "Squirrel" reading a book, oblivious to its sinking. (Thus ended the life of the man who set England on her course of colonising America.)

Walter Raleigh assumed the mantle of heir-presumptive to his late brother's ambitions; generously, he placed his energies and private resources at the disposal of the English bid to settle North America. On April 27th. 1584, he sent Captains Barlowe and Amidas to explore the mainland near Ocracock Island, off the coast of what is now North Carolina. Their descriptions of cedar forests abundant with deer, hares and fowl of all kinds, plus their account of the peaceful Indian village they had seen at Roanoke Island, was enough to encourage seven ships to land there in 1585—complete with over one hundred "householders and everything necessary to begin a new state."

The Admiral of the Fleet, Sir Richard Grenville returned to England and told Raleigh that all seemed to be well in the colony. They had begun to build on Roanoke Island and their neighbourly Indians had responded so readily to Christianity and The Bible that "many would be glad to touch it, to embrace it, to hold to their breasts and heads, and stroke all over their bodies with it!" But Thomas Heriot, the official secretary of the expedition saw it quite differently. He wrote that the new settlers were not at all suited to the tasks and rigours of colonising; they proved to be brawlers, quite ignorant of farming and basic survival; individuals more inclined to be adventurers and "covetors of fortune" as opposed to peaceful and hardworking, dedicated colonists. (Heriot is accorded the dubious honour of being the discoverer of tobacco, samples of which he sent back for Raleigh to inspect and smoke.)

The colony was destined for failure. As a parting gesture, Grenville had burnt an Indian village, thereby leaving the new settlers to face a winter of native hostilities as well as the harshness of a strange climate and tragic food shortages. The next year, they all hitched a lift back to England when Drake sailed by with one of his fleets. In doing so, they narrowly missed Grenville returning with more provisions. Confused at finding the colony abandoned, he detailed fifteen of his men to stay behind—and back he went to Raleigh.

In 1587, another group arrived. They landed at Hatorask (Cape Hatteras) on 22nd. July and went straight to Roanoke to confer with Grenville's men; but none were ever found.

Under the charge of Governor John White and a Council of twelve, the new arrivals began rebuilding the settlement. One encouraging sign was the safe birth of the first child to be born in America of European parentage—Virginia, whose mother was Governor White's daughter Eleanor, the wife of Ananias Dare.

Brimming with optimism, White was back in England conferring with Walter Raleigh in 1588. Even though this was the year of the Armada, they managed to release two boats, load them with provisions and send them on their way. But this good promise soon turned sour; the crews mutinied, turned to piracy and never reached the colonists. By the time that White was ready to leave in 1589, Raleigh had filled three ships with seeds, food and general merchandise which were in desperate shortage. Mysteriously, however, neither White nor his Roanoke settlers were ever seen again. With customary loyalty, Raleigh continued searching for them even up to 1602—but they were never found.

The utopian goals of colonisation again fell unfertilised; the derelict fields of Virginia lay fallow, weeds grew unmolested and seedlings of fir and cedar again took root in the abandoned soil.

All of this had taken place in 1589, the same year that Drake was failing to place Don Antonio onto the Portuguese throne; the same year that Sir George Somers had returned with such glory and wealth aboard "Flibcoate," from The Azores.

It is pure speculation to suggest that Sir George Somers gradually became committed to the development of Virginia simply because of the influence of Sir Walter Raleigh. But there is no doubt that their long-standing friendship played a significant role in drawing him towards the doctrines of colonisation.

By the start of the seventeenth century, English social conditions had radically changed and colonies were being proposed as a partial solution to her problems. Unemployment was particularily high because of the rapid expansion of the woollen industry—a development which saw the conversion of farmland into pastures, and the redundancy of countless farmhands. The respective economists who advised both Elizabeth and then James I, each agreed that such critical levels of unemployment could be somewhat alleviated by sending these labourers to raise crops in Virginia. By doing this they could give themselves a fresh start in life, whilst simultaneously furnishing England with the additional foodstuffs which she now urgently needed to fend-off domestic shortages caused by this change-over of land use.

It was therefore quite appropriate that Sir George Somers was among those who sat in the Houses of Parliament when this entire issue was tabled for discussion in 1604. The topic had sprung quite naturally from another matter raised during the last years of Elizabeth. M.P.'s had begun to take issue with the Queen's practice of giving Letters of Patent to her favourites. Walter Raleigh had been given one which gave him the exclusive right to mining over most of Devon and Cornwall. It was argued that this was a monopoly; that it was unjust, inhibited competition and produced the high prices which were the source of so much displeasure in the country. Elizabeth had appointed a committee to investigate the feelings of her people towards such monopolies and to establish the precise effects which they had on the economic situation.

By 1604, the committee was ready to present its findings, under a new monarch altogether.

The debates provided a fascinating introduction to state business for George Somers. He was privileged to be in such noble company as Sir Francis Bacon—an acknowledged genius of his generation—and Sir Edwin Sandys, perhaps the greatest orator then serving in the House of Commons. As a seaman and business man, Sir George had been brought to testify before the special sub-committee chaired by Sir Edwin Sandys, one which also introduced him to such luminaries as Sir Thomas Smith and Sir Richard Hawkins, the ship-mate from Plymouth.

The debate on colonisation took two main positions. Firstly, it was maintained that the Royal Patents did grant total control over one commodity into the hands of a select few; prices were fixed and the public was helpless. The second, counter-point was that Free Trade Associations allowed a healthy spirit of competition and prices would inevitably go down. Sir George Somers was very aware that any policy which would stimulate more trading and discovery, would also be welcome encouragement for his constituents and he argued that most mariners had now grown tired of going to sea, to war. A voice to the rear of the chamber was driven to support his view, asking what there was for the sons of prominent gentlemen to do, if they didn't want to go to war? The patents and monopolies even denied them the chance of becoming successful merchants!

Throughout the parliamentary sessions of 1604 and 1605, Sir George Somers actively sat and participated in these discussions. He spoke from the floor of the House and served on committees. As a result of this common interest, he became very close to Sir Edwin Sandys and Sir Thomas Smith; in the next few years they would share many conversations, business deals and ales together.

In the House of Lords, well beyond Sir George's sphere of influence, the same issues were being debated, but because of the composition of those who sat in that Upper House, the emphasis was invariably quite different. The powerful clergy who sat and debated colonisation sought to inject awareness that those who eventually became colonists had an obligation to promote Christian principles. The Bible should be their spur, their driving force. Ad nauseum they quoted from endless expeditions over the previous thirty years which had carried this awareness in the form of priests, men who had fearlessly advanced to face "the primitives," Bibles defiantly thrust forwards as shields.

They cited the glowing memory of Rev. Thomas Wolfall who had gone with Sir Martin Frobisher in 1578 "the onely care he had to save soules and to reforme those Infidels if it were possible!" They recalled the service which Rev. Francis Fletcher had conducted on the shores of the Pacific Ocean with Francis Drake in 1579 and "prayed the Almighty God to open their blinded eyes"—probably watched by the bewildered natives who peeped from the undergrowth! Month after month the churchmen sent echoes along the corridors of the House of Lords, words of "compassion for the poore Infidels captivated by the Deveill."

After close to two years of such preachings, their point was well made. They too went on record as supporting a policy of colonisation for America, so long as their quest to spread The Word was also noted.

The final argument to be presented was that by creating these free Trading Companies, not only would healthy competition result, and prices fall, but the increased activity would also see more goods being imported into England—and therefore more taxes for the Royal Account. The remark tipped the scales. Having inherited an enormous debt from Elizabeth, James was falling deeper and deeper into the chasm of insolvency at the annual rate of 100,000 pounds per year. The thought of getting more money into the treasury via import taxes was instantly appealing to him.

In 1605, both Houses approved a Bill which encouraged groups of investors to create new Trading Companies. One of the first to apply for a Royal Charter for formation was The Virginia Company. Raleigh's fragile private efforts had changed into a nationwide corporate effort.

The Charter which James I granted on April 10th. 1606 was really a permit for two different groups of investors to explore and colonise two separate but adjacent areas in the vicinity of Virginia. One branch was based in London and included among its executive officers: Sir Thomas Gates, Sir George Somers, Edward-Maria Wingfield and Richard Hakluyt. (Hakluyt was the representative of The Church and its designated Chaplain.)

This London-Virginia Company was described in the Charter of 1606 as "the first colony" and it was granted full rights to occupy and develop all of that area which lay between 34 degrees north and 41 degrees north: ". . . and that they shall have all the lands, woods, soil, grounds, havens, ports, rivers, mines, minerals, waters, fishings, commodities and hereditaments whatsoever by the space of fifty miles of English statue measure, all along the said coast of Virginia and America, towards the west and south-west, as on the coast lyeth, with all the islands within one hundred miles directly over against the said coast; and all the lands, soil, grounds, havens, ports, rivers . . . alongst the said coast of Virginia and America towards the east and north-east, or towards the north, as the coast lyeth, together with all the islands within one hundred miles, directly over against the said sea coast . . . and the same fifty miles every way on the sea coast, directly into the main land by a space of one hundred English miles . . ."

It was a gigantic, audacious land-grant encompassing thousands of square miles of a continent which was already happily occupied by its own native peoples. But such a consideration was quite irrelevant to both King James and those who received the first Virginia Company Charter. It was definitely a challenge, an undertaking of such a magnitude that there was no precedent. Never before had a group of private individuals been given the chance to start a new State in this manner.

(The "second colony" consisted of a group of investors based in Plymouth, Exeter and Bristol. Among others, it included George Popham, Thomas Hanham, Raleigh Gilbert and William Parker. Their land-grant, of similar proportions, was to the north of the other one and centred upon what is now Maine. Because they were partly in tandem, the two colonial regions overlapped slightly and it was presumed that they would probably converge at some future data.)

The Charter was very precise and clearly listed what was expected of all parties. It outlined obligations for establishing laws and maintaining order through Colonial Councils which, in turn would be supervised through a Council of Virginia, based in England. The needs for ensuring proper defences, correct planting and mining procedures were also explained and there was a lengthy section prescribing the Official Seals for specific functionaries. There was a section noting the basic supplies which the settlers were entitled to have at their disposal—weapons, furniture and gunpowder. Another clause covered trading rights and obligations—particularly the prohibition of directly trading with foreign countries and their colonies. Another sub-section guaranteed the safeguarding of rights and privileges which the colonists and any of their subsequent children could expect to enjoy.

On November 20th. 1606 King James appointed his Council for Virginia.

On 19th. December, less than a month later, Captain Christopher Newport led the London-Virginia Company's first three boats up the Thames Estuary. The permanent colonisation of Virginia was finally underway.

14

The Ways To Virginia

The departure of the Virginia Company's first fleet, on 19th. December 1606, was an exhilarating spectacle orchestrated to match the natural pre-Christmas air of gaiety and festivity. As soon as the tide rose to its highwater mark against the quayside of London's Blackwall dock, Captain Christopher Newport gave the command to hoist anchors and unfurl canvas. Crowds lined the wharf to witness the start of this historic undertaking. Some waved scarves and hats; others bowed their heads in silent sorrow, weeping, unable to take a last look at the apprehensive faces of their departing kith and kin.

Somers, Gates and Newport had been huddled together throughout much of the previous night, discussing last-minute details and trying to exhaust foreseeable problems. Captain Bartholomew Gosnold had meanwhile taken over the responsibility for making final checks of the expedition's provisions, organising crews and passengers. At dawn he pronounced that all was complete and ready to depart.

By envoy, King James had sent his personal good wishes for a successful voyage, urging the settlers to work together and through their unity bring the inevitable "infidels and savages" into the Christian brotherhood of good government and "human civilisation." From the upper deck, Captain Newport proclaimed his hopes that the venture would bring fame and prosperity to the settlers, the Company and, last but not least, "his majesties revenue." It was a practical and diplomatic seaman's speech, the last words of which gradually petered-out amidst shouts and cheers.

Steadily and in file, the three boats made their way up into the Thames Estuary and then headed along the English Channel. The lead boat was "Susan Constant," a vessel of one hundred tons and carrying seventy-one persons, including Newport. Closely behind came Captain Gosnold aboard "Godspeed," a vessel of forty tons which appeared to be slightly overcrowded with its fifty-two passengers and crew. To the rear came the nifty "Discovery," a smaller ship of just twenty-one tons but which slipped easily through the waters under the care and guidance of Captain John Ratcliffe. He had most of the supplies which would be needed once they arrived in Virginia, and a compliment of twenty people. In all the expedition consisted of thirty-nine crewmen and about one-hundred-and-five "planters"—half of whom had been classified as "gentlemen" and the rest as "labourers, merchants and trademen." Also in the party were Captain John Smith and the Church's ambassador Preacher Robert Hunt.

Everyone was optimistic. George Somers and the other investors had been particularly inspired by reports of large quantities of gold being located only the year before by an expedition under Sir John Zouch, Henry Wriothesley and Bryan Cave of Bristol. At the forefront of their minds must have been the possibility of a quick return for their money, as opposed to long-term rewards. But no sooner had they disappeared beyond the cliffs of southern England than they encountered storms which forced them to seek refuge inland for a further week. It was therefore not until the start of January 1607 that they managed to head out into the open ocean. Following the traditional southern route via the Canaries, at 4 a.m. on Sunday 28th. April that they reached the coast of Virginia.

On May 13th. they sailed up Chesapeake Bay and landed at the spot chosen as the site for Jamestown. A month later, Rev. Hunt celebrated 'The Comfortable Sacrament of the Last Supper'—an offering of thanks which might well have been primarily for his own benefit as opposed to everyone else. The thirty-eight-year-old minister had previously served in the decidedly quieter surroundings of a small village in Kent; unused to this type of seafaring ministry he had been consistently and violently sick throughout the entire voyage. Thankful to be offering landed thanks he most certainly was!

Almost immediately, Captain Newport was preparing to return to England. Behind him he left an authorised Council of Government, although they eventually argued and total power was assumed by Captain John Smith—at that time a young soldier only twenty-eight years of age.

The Virginia Company eagerly listened to Newport's account of the venture and there was general satisfaction that there had not been any disastrous mishaps to report. They took heed of his remark that during the short time that he had remained in Virginia, he considered most of the settlers to be quite "ill-fitted to subdue the wilderness." It was an observation which they would bear in mind for the selection of the next batch of emmigrants.

Meanwhile, preparations were instantly undertaken to re-equip the fleet and send it directly back again to Jamestown. Captain Newport was soon heading westwards and he landed in Virginia on 14th. January 1608.

Superficially, everything seemed to be progressing quite favourably. Captain Smith had consolidated his power and was already making overtures to the neighbouring Indian tribes. But beneath the thin veneer grumblings and dis-satisfaction were quick to surface at the slightest provocation, so that this mood was hastily passed on to the latest arrivals; and they started their new lives in gloom.

Towards the end of January, shortly after Newport had returned, a fire swept through the encampment destroying one of the main buildings which contained general provisions, and also the church. As if in humble repayment for having been given the energy to rebuild his church, the luckless Rev. Hunt completed his task, offered thanks and dropped dead. (His will was taken back and probated in London on 14th. July 1608.)

But the overall tone of the new colony was hardly downcast. There was undoubtedly determination to succeed and although for many the transition from city-dweller to backwoodsman was arduous and painful, most tackled their appointed tasks with genuine effort. Newport was especially elated to fill his boat "John and Francis" with vast quantities of iron-ore, sassafras roots, cedar posts and walnut wood. Such an unexpected haul could do nothing but excite the shareholders in London and encourage them to expand the colony even more. (Valued at 4 pounds per ton on the London market, the iron-ore on its own was a fine return for the investors. The sassafras root was also highly regarded in some circles since it possessed comforting properties for those inflicted with venereal diseases.)

By and large, these first years of the Virginia Company had been rewarding beyond expectations. But, of course, there was realistic acceptance that considerable work was still required by both London and Virginia before the colony could be left to stand on its own. Each trip had exposed serious needs and deficiencies and made further trips from England a continuing and urgent necessity. The colonists needed a variety of specific supplies—and sometimes sat waiting impatiently for them to arrive from England.

Food and health continued to be the priorities. Few had been totally prepared for the far harsher and longer winters of North America; they were not always physically and mentally capable of handling such inclement conditions. It remained a disturbing fact that only about half of each new group of settlers was still alive and well after the first year. And during the bitter months of winter, people sat in the dark insides of their wooden homes, huddled over smoking wood fires, brooding, plotting; trying to work out a way of making themselves more comfortable and happier. Deaths were common from disease, hunger and Indian attacks. A gallant London dandy was supremely inept in the arts of tracking deer during a snowstorm, just as a farmhand from Essex was incompetent when it came to hand-to-hand combat with an Indian wielding a tomahawk.

When Newport returned to England in 1608, "Sea Venture" was on the brink of completion and it was decided that a major relief expedition should be sent out to Virginia within a year in order to try to stabilise and improve the living conditions of the colonists. (There was, afterall, a fully-detailed commitment which the original Charter had imposed upon The Company. London had an obligation to tend to the needs of the settlers; Virginia had a right to expect it.)

By the end of 1608, things were far from desperate in Jamestown, although even from the security of London it was perfectly obvious that the settlement could not survive if completely neglected. Remarkable inroads had been accomplished. The colony was still surviving after three winters and Smith was undeniably making progress in his relationship with the neighbouring tribes—a task greatly eased as a result of his own relationship with the attractive and appealing daughter of Chief Powhatan, a young woman named Pocahontas. The continuing loss of life remained a major obstacle to be confronted and solved; health was a problem—Captain Bartholomew Gosnold had died there during 1607—and it was realised that something had to be done to encourage the emigration of medical persons, doctors with the same willingness to tend to the bodies of the settlers in the way that preachers were eager to minister to their souls.

As preparations got underway for the relief fleet of 1609, these topics were forever in everyone's minds. They all knew deep-down that the threat of the Indian could be significantly minimised if only they could side-step mutual provocations. Captain Newport had himself confirmed from first-hand experience that "they are a very witty and ingenious people, apt to both understand and speake o'r language." Peace was a matter which could be solved with diplomacy and trinket-gifts; failing that, then a garrison of musketmen could always be stationed in Jamestown to do the job of enforcing peace!

On the basis of both knowledge and experience, the members of the 1606 Charter for The Virginia Company began to look ahead at the future. They foresaw a time when they would need to increase the flow of cash, people and "victuals" in proportions beyond their existing capabilities; they envisaged a point when they would have to expand and restructure the economy and social order of the entire region. They therefore approached King James with a petition seeking to renegotiate their terms of reference and pave the way for a more appropriate Second Charter.

Sir George Somers was now devoting more and more of his time to the affairs of the Virginia Company. It was a pre-occupation which resulted in his being more often in London than he was ever able to be in Dorset. Time spent with Joane grew as short as the daylight hours of winter. Living in the seclusion of Berne Manor with only the company of her servants, she must have already begun to know what it would be like as a widow.

Matthew had recently married Joan Roope and with the birth of their daughter Elizabeth, his visits out to Whitchurch had become noticeably infrequent. His brother Nicholas was now in his mid-twenties and preparing to similarily settle-down and raise a family. Sir George's brother John was still living in Lyme Regis but business rarely afforded him the spare time to ride out to visit with his sister-in-law at Berne. He, of course, also had his own sizeable family to take care of: William, Toby and Mary were all grown-up and John had been married for a couple of years by now. Even cousin Robert Somers never paid a call on Lady Joane; his wife was expecting their first child sometime in August of 1609 and the bouncy journey to the other side of Charmouth was far more than might be reasonably expected of either him or his wife. What she did to alleviate the boredom of being alone we do not know; maybe she sat dutifully in the long room, quietly sewing or doing a tapestry for the fire-screen. Perhaps she sat contentedly reading Richard Hakluyt's "Principal Navigations," using the printed word to take her to the exciting places which her husband always spoke of when he returned from a voyage. Certainly there is nothing to show that she ever thought to dabble in the more errant ways of a single, lonely socialite.

It was probably during the Christmas recess of Parliament that Sir George informed his wife of his decision to go to Virginia with the Company's fleet in 1609. After this time, he was intimately involved more-or-less full-time with the details and logistics of the voyage. For the future of Virginia, The Company and English colonial intentions in North America, this would be a most crucial expedition.

Once the decision was made, he had to immediately extricate himself from other distractions. Within Lyme Regis, his activities as a participating member of the Town Council had already begun to dwindle and after 1607 his name no longer features on a regular basis. That year, Walter Tucker had been made Mayor, with Sir George still serving as a common councillor; after his term elapsed, Anthony Moore was appointed to the office and Sir George was by now making only occasional attendances at their meetings.

A second position which he had to consider relinquishing was his more exalted seat as Member of Parliament for Lyme Regis. This was a post which he had begun to enjoy with more and more pleasure; he liked the atmosphere of the House of Commons, rose to the challenges of debates and was admired and respected by his parliamentary colleagues. But when it became public knowledge that he would be absent from his duties for an indefinite period of time whilst away in 'The Colonies,' his future as a political figure was instantly thrown into doubt. In the first session in the House of Commons for 1609, he found his predicament to be the subject of a single debate. There was no precedent. It was unique to have an M.P. taking a leave-of-absence which might protract itself for as much as a year, or even more; in one sense, this alone technically inferred that he had vacated his seat of his own accord. On the other hand, his absence was plainly in the name of a cause which they had so lustily debated in that very same chamber just a year or so earlier. His absence could hardly be mistaken for some idle, leisurely vacation. Sir George Somers was a popular figure and the debate was often in his favour, as colleague after colleague rose to argue his support. It was pointed-out that he was making a voyage which could be highly beneficial to their own future deliberations, one which could furnish them with a real, practical assessment of the effectiveness of their own ideas and policies. He could report back to the main body or one of the committees and offer an evaluation of the entire development of the colonial doctrine.

But popularity and diverse shades of argument were not sufficient to secure majority support. Although he had enjoyed the eloquent help of Sir Edwin Sandys among others it was decreed that the actual length of his anticipated absence constituted the voluntary act of vacating his own parliamentary seat. By going to Virginia in 1609, Sir George was thereby relinquishing his position as M.P. for Lyme Regis. He was unaminously wished "Good luck and God speed!"

By the early Spring, he had successfully managed to settle his local and national responsibilities. Furthermore, his diminishing role within the family business was readily handled by brother John. Domestically, Lady Somers had long since resigned herself to being left alone; as a married woman without children this was her destiny.

Stripped of any external distractions, he was now able to give full attention to The Virginia Company; more specifically, the upcoming expedition and the new Charter.

The financing of such a major undertaking had been a gargantuan task, one which occupied a considerable amount of time over the previous eighteen months. With Sir Edwin Sandys and Sir Thomas Smith he had exploited individual and collective connections to the utmost, for their fund-raising efforts. They had solicited among the Nation's wealthiest patrons, trading companies, guilds and a variety of associations. Additionally, private citizens had been given the opportunity to purchase shares in the Company at a rate of slightly more than twelve pounds apiece. The response had been overwhelming and by the time that the Second Charter was brought into effect they had secured the backing of 662 individuals and 55 different groups. Among their ranks were 8 Earls, 12 Lords, 96 Knights and a miscellaneous collection of sailors, grocers, ministers, aristocrats and merchants. There were also two foreign shareholders, the Jacobsons of Antwerp.

The list of those who had contributed to The Virginia Company read like an Elizabethan version of "Who's Who?" Among them were: Sir William Herbert, the Earl of Pembroke; Sir Henry Wriothesley, the Earl of Southampton; Sir Robert Cecil, the Earl of Salisbury; Sir Amayas Preston; Sir Francis Bacon; Sir Thomas West, Lord de la Warr; Sir Thomas Gresham and the Lord Mayor of London. Sir Thomas Smith and Sir George Somers were also shareholders and Sir Edwyn Sandys must have lobbied heavily into his own family, for there were many of his relatives on the list. Another investor was Lord Mounteagle, the hero of the Gunpowder Plot. Richard Hakluyt was on the list, as were Daniel Tucker, Arthur Pett and Nicholas Ferrar. (Tucker and Ferrar were destined to make indelible impressions on the development of Bermuda and Virginia respectively.) Among the seamen who bought shares were Captain John Smith; Captain Edward-Maria Wingfield; Captain John Ratcliffe; Captain William Winter and Captain Thomas Wyat.

This astounding increase in capital provided the Virginia Company with the cash flow required to equip a large fleet for 1609. It further enabled the Company to purchase extensive provisions and supplies which in turn would allow the colony to truly expand to the fullness of its potential. In order to legally permit such changes and expansion, the holders of the original Charter petitioned King James for a completely revised Second Charter. After an exhaustive passage through endless committees and boards of advisors, it was formally granted on 23rd. May 1609.

The document noted that the original adventurers and planters had already engaged in the business of the colony and had now reached the point where there was an obvious need to reach beyond the limitations imposed by the original Charter. In almost nine-thousand words, twenty-nine clauses set out to do just that. The borders of the area were defined as stretching two hundred miles both north and south of Cape Comfort; jurisdiction was given over all islands lying within one hundred miles of the coast, plus further territories inland. The 1609 Charter identified rights and liberties and reaffirmed the codes of conduct and obligations of each settler. There is clear mention of The Crown's right to one-fifth of all mined ores. Each shareholder is named. Other clauses relate to forms of government which are to be created in each community; how each will conduct itself and liase with the parent Council in England. Appointments are defined, alongside provisions for replacing appointees. England was also to retain the ultimate veto over who should be allowed to become a resident, as well as the religious complexion of Virginia.

It was totally comprehensive, left nothing ambiguous. All perimeters were precisely defined. It was a highly significant document which symbolised the end of an era when men pooled their private resources for a quick trip of exploration or privateering. This marked the introduction of proper business corporations, in which individuals invested money and became shareholders. Their investments were not for just one voyage, but for the development of the Company as a whole. Under the Second Charter, the group was now officially named: "The Treasurer and Company of Adventurers and Planters of the City of London for the First Colony of Virginia." The paperwork had been drawn-up by legal expert Edwin Lukin—whose confidence was such that he purchased some shares for himself.

"Sea Venture" had already been launched earlier in the year and lay at anchor in Plymouth Sound. A month after King James granted The Virginia Company its second Charter, the 1609 relief fleet was ready to sail.

Merchants of Virginia.

EN DAY VIRGINIA QVINTAM

THe Company of Merchants, called *Merchants of Virginia.*

A page from Stow's "Survey of London," 1633. Showing
the Arms of The London Company.

15

The Relief Fleet Disaster Of 1609

Because of the importance and size of the Relief Fleet, its imminent departure in 1609 attracted widespread interest and publicity.

An article appeared in the February edition of "Nova Brittania" praising the work of The Virginia Company and outlining its plans for the future; another piece was featured in "Good Speed" on 25th. April, giving the objectives of the 'Somers Fleet' and wishing it well. Churches too resounded with prayers and sermons to guide them on their way. On 21st. February the Rev. William Crashaw had given a sermon directly to leading members of The Virginia Company, concluding with: "I have prayed for thee that thy faith fail not." Similar words of hope and support were delivered by Dr. Symonds during a service in London's White Chapel, on April 25th. and in another offered by the Rev. Price of Paul Cross, on May 28th.

Meanwhile, the passengers themselves had made their ways to appointed departure ports. The bulk of the fleet planned to leave from the London dock at Woolwich, pausing at Plymouth to gather another two boats. Opinion varies considerably as to the suitability of the passengers to become colonists and it is obvious that at least some of them were aboard only because they volunteered and paid—rather than because they had been selected for their virtues and attributes.

Captain George Percy, who sailed with them and remained in Virginia long enough to be appointed Deputy Governor in 1610, was of the opinion that the passengers were "divers gentlemen, sowldiers and seaman" and seemed mildly impressed by the group as a whole; historian J. H. Latane agrees and, asserts that they were "persons of ranke and qualitie." This is not the opinion of researcher E. Clowes Chorley, however. In an article published in 1930 he quotes an unsigned document written by one of the colonists who observes that they were: "poore gentlemen, tradesmen, serving men, libertines and such like, ten times more fit to spoil a commonwealth, than either begin one."

They certainly included in their midst many shareholders in the Company. On board the "Sea Venture" alone there were at least eight passengers with a vested interest in the fleet's good fortunes—Sir George Somers, Sir Thomas Gates, Sir George Yeardley, Captain Newport, Henry Shelly, James Swift and Thomas Whittingham all owned shares. Somers had also conducted at least some partial screening of those who would travel on his ship and he knew that Francis Pearepoint and Jeffrey Breare (Briars) were from respected Dorset families. He was even willing to allow reformed shareholder Silvester Jourdain to join them! His nephew Matthew was made an officer aboard "Swallow."

In addition to loading the boats with food for the trip and provisions for those already in Virginia, the Virginia Company was thoughtfully mindful of other needs and made sure that a supply of books and other reading material was available. Bible, prayer books, "books of piety" and various practical handbooks were placed on board, alongside two books regarded by Sir Thomas Smith as being quite indispensible: Richard Hakluyt's "Principal Navigations" and a 1602 version of John Bereton's "Discoverie of Virginia." All reading material had been carefully classified and compiled by Ferrar, the man who would become Virginia's resident recorder, who stated: "some good book always in store being in solitude the best and choicest company."

Each Captain also placed a selection of maps and charts in his cabin, a variety made absolutely necessary by the frequent inaccuracies over distances and locations of places. Of special value in the waters of the West Atlantic were: Michael Lok's Polar Map of North America (1582); Edward Wright's "Hydrographical Map" (1599); the White-De Bry map of the Chesapeake Bay area of Virginia, printed in 1590. Spanish maps also contained valuable reference points for navigators, especially those by Alonso de Santa Cruz (1536/45); Juan Martinez (1589) and

Filips Galle (1587). Each of these had been recently reissued for the benefit of seaman travelling across the Atlantic. Each, as it so happened, located Bermuda.

Excitement mounted when Captain Samuel Argylle sailed from Portsmouth on 5th. May. He had been commissioned to conduct a study of fishing in and around the Virginia coastline, but had also been given the task of trying to establish a more suitable route directly to Virginia, instead of taking the longer and more common course which caused boats to go head into the West Indies before turning up along the coast of America. His voyage was not related to that of the relief fleet although he did reach Jamestown nine weeks later and forwarded news that Sir George Somers himself would be heading the party due to follow shortly.

On 15th. May 1609, 7 ships left Woolwich and reached Plymouth on May 20th. These were: "Falcon," "Blessing," "Unitie," "Lion," "Swallow," "Catch" and "Virginia." At Plymouth they joined "Diamond" and Sir George Somers' ship "Sea Venture."

"Sea Venture" was the new pride and joy of Lyme Regis and people had come to look at her laying at anchor in Plymouth Sound. She was about to make her maiden trans-Atlantic voyage having only recently been launched. But each of the other boats had its tales to tell. "Swallow" had seen action under Sir Richard Hawkins, in the famous Armada campaign; "Blessing" had sailed many times into the Caribbean and would still be carrying colonists out to Virginia and Bermuda ten years later. "Diamond" was a Lyme Regis boat owned by Robert Henley of Colway Manor and in 1608 had just returned from one trip to Newfoundland and another down to Spain and Portugal.

After completing the loading of an estimated 10,000 lbs. of beef and a stock of biscuits onto "Sea Venture," the fleet was ready. Sir George Somers' vessel was one of the larger boats (300 tons) and had plenty of space for provisions; "Catch" and "Virginia" were the two smallest in the fleet and were being taken to Virginia as supply boats. "Sea Venture" was captained by Christopher Newport and, in addition to Sir George Somers—Admiral of this fleet—it also carried Sir Thomas Gates, the Lieutenant-Governor of Virginia and Sir George Yeardley, the Commander of the Land Forces. On hindsight, it was foolish to have placed them on the same ship; their loss would be catastrophic.

Late on the evening of 2nd. June 1609, the tide rose to its high-water mark and in the setting sun the Relief Fleet finally departed.

William Strachey reports that the fleet tried to maintain visual contact with each boat as they cut through the relatively calm waters of the eastern Atlantic. But after seven weeks everything suddenly changed. On Monday July 24th., when they were about 1,000 miles west of The Azores and lying at a latitude of 27 degrees north, they were hit by a storm. From descriptions, it was probably one of the notorious freak conditions which plague this area. Dark, swirling cumulo-nimbus clouds descended around them, causing powerful gusts of wind to rip into their sails. The seas became choppy and dangerous; the pointed crests of the waves were whipped into foam and then blasted into tattered spray. Captains bellowed ill-heard commands; crew held-on, pulled ropes, slipped and tried again.

The fleet was completely scattered. From the rear decks of "Sea Venture," Sir George Somers caught a glimpse of the small pinnace "Catch" and managed to get a rope to it before she might be sunk by some dangerous rogue wind. Together the two ships were bounced and battered for the rest of that day and through the night; the storm was showing no signs of abating. It continued for the whole of Tuesday, at which time Captain Newport was receiving word from his crew that they had sprung a leak beneath deck. Somers and Gates went below to check; their worst fears were confirmed—the "Sea Venture" was now in critical danger of sinking.

Fearing that it was doing neither ship any good, indeed being fastened together had now become a dangerous menace, the order was given to cut "Catch" free. It was the last contact which anyone would ever have with Captain Michael Philes and his crew. In England there would be more widows and orphans.

The storm continued—"clouds gathering upon us, the winds singing and whistling"—the beleaguered boat and its crew grew colder, wetter; despondant. For a full three days they endured the malicious weather, days in which they bailed relentlessly, trying to keep afloat; trying to keep the water out before more worked its way through the splintering hull. Throughout, Sir George Somers took his turn at bailing in the swampy darkness below; Sir Thomas Gates stood at his side, with Yeardley, Newport, Thomas Powell, Nicholas Bennett, Henry Ravens, Silvester Jourdain . . . they each played their part. Elizabeth Person and Mistress Eason tended the needs of the injured, helped to comfort the pain of blistered hands and exhaustion. The Rev. Richard Bucke, the Church's replacement for Richard Hakluyt, bailed and suffered with them; praying, seeking divine help. Calling them to have Faith. Meanwhile passengers vomitted, slithered through the puked mess on the floor of their sleeping quarters. The sailors and their officers were troubled but orderly; they'd had storms before—although the screeching panic of the other passengers made them all unsettled.

Even William Strachey, a well-seasoned traveller of some note, admits that he started to think the worst. The leaks had been partially repaired, but a lot of caulking had been lost and Captain Newport was uncertain as to how long they could manage to remain afloat. In shifts they pumped-out the water, three groups taking it in turn, but there remained the perpetual danger that the boat might overturn. On Thursday, the order was given to toss superfluous luggage over the side, with unnecessary beer, wine and other bulky items. But still they bailed, thousands of gallons each day.

Finally, on Friday 28th. July land was sighted. Instinctively, Sir George knew that this would be The Bermudas. He had not dared to hope that they could find them under these tortuous conditions but he did know that they were in this part of the Atlantic—had sailed by them some years before; had even entertained using them as part of a future route between London and Virginia. But now it was as if Providence had suddenly dropped those islands there, so clearly visible and so close.

Captain Newport steered his battered boat towards the complex pattern of reefs which encircle the islands; Somers high on the bow helping to guide and direct him. When not a mile from the shore, they grounded themselves in a gap in the coral and crunched to a halt. Without loss of life they were all safe. The Rev. Bucke offered thanks.

The remarkable maiden voyage of "Sea Venture" had come to an abrupt close and as she gently nudged herself deeper and deeper into the coral reef, the relieved crew and passengers ferried whatever could be salvaged on the crescent-shaped beach which lay close to where it was perched. Then, over the next few days they watched from the safety of the sands until she had finally slipped from sight, into the clear waters of her tomb.

The lives which these shipwrecked survivors led, whilst marooned on Bermuda for the next ten months, has been carefully and often repeated in books and journals.

We know that there were some initial problems over the question of authority and command. Sir George Somers was of the opinion that as Admiral of the Fleet, he was totally responsible for ensuring that all of them reached their destination in Virginia. Since they were still not yet there, he presumed himself to still have that responsibility and authority. On the other hand, Sir Thomas Gates was keen to remark that he was afterall the Lieutenant-Governor of the entire colony, making his way to take up his temporary appointment until Lord de la Warre arrived in 1610. As such, he argued, now that they were on land he was responsible. Captain Newport was tactfully apart from this discrete haggling; he was Captain of "Sea Venture" and was now without his command.

Just how public this issue over authority became is unclear. Obviously everyone was delighted to have survived both storm and shipwreck, but they were equally as concerned about what their precise futures might be, now that they had managed to land on a totally deserted island. Sir George evidently backed-off from more arguing and the three leaders divided their efforts into three distinct areas of concern: Sir George Somers under-took to provide for their food needs; Captain Newport would begin to work on the construction of another vessel which would enable them to complete their journey. Sir Thomas Gates assumed command of housing—plus the day-to-day problems of living. In effect, he also held the reigns of power.

In the meanwhile, the rest of the Relief Fleet had eventually straggled its way up to Jamestown. "Falcon," "Blessing," "Unitie" and "Lion" arrived virtually together, on August 11th. The passengers and crew aboard "Unitie" had experienced particularily unpleasant conditions on board and when she finally dropped anchor in Chesapeake Bay there were very few of them who were not ill. Her Master, Captain Arthur Pett, was critically ill and made his will on 30th. August. A shareholder in the Virginia Company, the trip had begun for him as one of adven-ture, but by now the joy had long since faded. He was trans-ferred onto "Blessing" and placed under the care of Captain Robert Adams, but he never recovered and died. In the middle of August, "Diamond" and "Virginia" arrived; but their story was no less pleasant. The smallest boat to survive the storm, "Vir-ginia" was dangerously battered and in desperate need of repairs. "Diamond" had lost its mainstay in the storm and barely managed to limp to safety; her passengers and crew had also to fight an outbreak of disease on board and most of them were already dead. The last boat to arrive in Virginia was "Swallow" with Matthew Somers still standing firmly by the side of Captain George Percy; they too had suffered seasick crew and passen-gers and the boat was damaged.

They discovered the Virginia colonists to be in only slightly better condition than were the remnants of the newly-arrived fleet. Without the provisions which they had been so desperately awaiting and relying on, the future looked bleak indeed. In September, John Smith was seriously injured by an explosion of gunpowder which ripped his stomach and thigh into a pulpy mess. It was decided that he should return with the most seaworthy vessels to England and file a full report with the Virginia Council in London; to let them know about the dreadful fate of the Relief Fleet and the deteriorating conditions at Jamestown.

Among the ships which returned to England was "Blessing," under Captain Adams, and "Lion" commanded by Captain Thomas Johnson. When they reached Plymouth in early March of 1610, they therefore became the bearers of the news about the fate of Sir George Somers and those aboard "Sea Venture." London was shocked and stunned. Adams also probated the will which had been handed to him by Captain Pett—his wife Florence and their young daughter Elizabeth would now never go to Virginia and start the new life which they had so often discussed.

In Bermuda, the power-sharing had worked with considerable success. Consistent and regular supplies of fish had been kept in store, as well as birds, eggs, various berries and vast quantities of wild hog. Sir George Somers and his group of men had worked without rest to make sure that they all eat well. Under the direction of Christopher Newport, one boat was reaching completion ("Deliverance") and Sir George had undertaken to build another to carry another to carry extra food and supplies. This would be named "Patience." Essentially, the small settlement which they had erected on St. George's Island had fared through the winter with no serious problems. Indeed, there was even a prevailing feeling that perhaps they might remain in Bermuda and not continue to Virginia as originally intended. But Sir Thomas Gates repeated his intention of fullfilling their commitment by going to Jamestown. Then, if circumstances made it possible, they could perhaps be freed to return to Bermuda at another date. Until such time, however, Sir Thomas remained adamant about their obligations to The Company as well as his own commitment to the colony of Virginia.

Life in Bermuda had been eventful. They had had a murder (Edward Samuel killed by Robert Waters); an execution (Henry Paine, for 'sedition'); and a marriage—Thomas Powell, Sir George's servant had married Elizabeth Persons, the maidservant of Mistress Horton. They had even experienced the joy of having two births: on 11th. February 1610, a daughter named Bermuda had been born to John Rolfe and his wife; followed by a baby boy named Bermudas, the child of Mr. and Mrs. Edward

Eason. And there had also been deaths—Jeffrey Breare, Richard Lewis, William Hitchman, and the tiny Rolfe baby. In his records of this episode, Nicholas Ferrar also states that Lady Gates, wife of Sir Thomas, was in Bermuda and that she died here too.

The stranded community had even experienced its own piece of local intrigue—thanks to the provocations of a religious zealot named Stephen Hopkins. Made official clerk to the Rev. Bucke, he seems to have got carried away with his duties and on 24th. January was made to stand trial before Sir Thomas on the charge that he had tried to forment dissention by persuading Sam Sharpe and Humphrey Reed that "no man should be made to go against his wishes." He had engaged them in a lofty conversation on rights and the obligation which husbands had towards their own families . . . that they could never be free in Virginia, if they were slaves to the Company . . . and so on. The tribunal sentenced him to death, but he was reprieved.

On 30th. March, they launched "Deliverance" and toward the end of April "Patience" had been completed and was ready to sail.

During the preceding months, Sir George Somers had also made the first detailed map of these islands and had expressed his interest in perhaps undertaking their development. He envisaged returning to London and gathering enough backers to start preliminary feasability studies. In conjunction with these private considerations, Sir Thomas Gates noted that they had a need to claim the territory formally for The Crown by retaining a presence on the islands until they could return to stake a more permanent claim.

Christopher Carter and Robert Waters agreed to remain whilst the rest continued to Virginia. And so it was that as soon as a favourable westerly wind blew across those sub-tropical islands, Sir George Somers and Christopher Newport carefully guided their homemade boats along a channel through the reef. It was ten o'clock in the morning and as they floated over the horizon two lonely figures waved from the shore.

According to Strachey's account, they kept a southerly course for the first few days and nervously lost sight of Sir George and "Patience" at least twice. By midnight of 18th. May they began to take depth-findings and confirmed that the water was getting shallower, that they were crossing onto the off-shore continental shelf of North America. At daybreak on May 21st. they sighted land and dropped anchor off Cape Henry.

Sitting on adjacent Cape Comfort was Captain George Percy.

Since reaching Virginia with the scattered fleet a year earlier, he had established an advance look-out atop the cape. That morning he was gazing despondently at the sea when on "the next tide we saw two pinnaces coming into the bay; not knowing yet what they were, we watched a boat coming from one of them and one of the watchguards hailed and called them and discovered that Sir Thomas Gates and Sir George Somers had come." At first, Somers was sceptical as to who occupied that small fortification on the cliff but upon learning that it was George Percy—who he knew well—they finally came into land; the next high tide they went up to Jamestown.

The ecstatic surprise and jubilation which greeted them at first soon subsided into sombre reality. At Jamestown they discovered the settlement to be close to ruins, the fortifications all broken down and the sixty inhabitants who were still alive "were scarce able to crawl out of their houses to greet the newcomers." Gates and Somers went straight to the delapidated and unfrequented church and the Rev. Bucke held a service of thanksgiving for their miraculous delivery.

But this was hardly the time to sit down and exchange stories. The deteriorating conditions of the colony more than eloquently conveyed the desperation into which the settlers had sadly descended. Sir Thomas Gates immediately assumed the position which he had been sent out to fill a year earlier; Sir George Somers undertook to assist the remains of the Virginia Council in taking stock of their supplies, ammunition; the "Sea Venture" passengers tried to inject some enthusiasm into the despair of the Jamestown survivors.

The evidence, however, was all too dampening. With considerable reluctance, the order was given to build caches for storing their weapons and tools; books and personal effects were carefully packed into chests; other items were buried beneath the floors of buildings. The sailors set about the task of making pitch and tar as caulking for their boats; women set about baking bread. The colony of Jamestown would be abandoned, they would return to England.

With considerably mixed feelings, a curdling of relief and defeat, they embarked for England. The sea Captains were again pleased to have the leadership of Sir George Somers and they unashamedly hovered about him, seeking his orders; pleased to be under his command once more. The administrators of the colony just as naturally flocked about Sir Thomas Gates for direction.

As Sir George Somers was slowly leading his mournful fleet up the Chesapeake Inlet, Lord de la Warre had just entered it with his three ships and an excited group of 150 additional immigrants. Unaware of any of the drama at Jamestown, or that Gates and Somers were alive and close at hand, he happily anchored off Cape Henry on the night of June 5th. One of the vessels with him was "Blessing" from the original Relief Fleet—now back in Virginia, under Sir Ferdinando Wayman.

The following morning, they were surprised to meet an advance-ship from the Somers fleet and, in the words of Lord de la Warre, it was "accompanied with the most happy news about the safe arrival of Sir George Somers and Sir Thomas Gates—sufficient to have broken my heart!"

After a joyful reunion in midstream, the majority of the ships turned back together to Jamestown. They landed on June 10th. 1610. The entire history of a continent was about to be reversed.

16

♟♟♟♟♟♟♟♟♟♟♟♟♟♟♟♟♟♟♟♟♟

The Last Voyage
To Bermuda

♟♟♟♟♟♟♟♟♟♟♟♟♟♟♟♟♟♟♟♟♟♟♟

Following a lengthy and exhaustive meeting of the Virginia Council a very thorough analysis was made of the colony's sorrowful state and a realistic evaluation was made with regards to the immediate future.

This first Council for Virginia met on 12th. June 1610. In addition to Lord de la Warre himself, it included Sir Thomas Gates, Captain Newport, Sir George Somers, Sir Ferdinando Wayman and Captain George Percy. With the exception of the latter two men, all of the others had recently arrived by way of Bermuda and the "Sea Venture" shipwreck. William Strachey acted as the official secretary and recorder for the proceedings.

Perhaps because he had barely had chance to set foot on land, and was therefore eager to enjoy at least some experiences as a colonist, Lord de la Warre very cleary indicated that he was in favour of them giving the project another year. But he was not aggressively insistent and welcomed independent testimony from others outside of the Council who cared to present an opinion. There was, of course, more than just a handful of the original settlers who had long-since decided that life in England was probably far less problematical than living in North America. They offered arguments for going back home, lavishly embellished with true stories of fights with marauding Indians. They described to their new Governor what it had been like to experience famine; to watch children die from swollen empty bellies and to endure endless weeks when the cold, still nights were forever being shattered by the screams and cries of those who were dying from some unexplainable disease. It had not been a pleasant period for them.

The most dejected members of the group presented tales of gloom and absolute hopelessness, painting a scenario in which there were always going to be bitterly cold winters when food supplies could never be expected to last for the entire season.

By contrast, those who had recently arrived from Bermuda were far more hardy and optimistic. Afterall, they were living proof of the ability to overcome astounding odds—and still thrive and be healthy. They were fairly united in a resolve to apply their collective experiences and prove that if they could manage to overcome life on a deserted island, then they could doubtless do just as well, if not better, on the mainland. They also argued that this had been their objective when they set-off a year earlier; it was what they still wanted to accomplish. One must, of course, remember that the power of argument was also supported by the weight of numbers; the "Sea Venture" passengers by now outnumbered the sixty or so half-starved settlers who had lived through that last tragic winter at Jamestown.

Lord De la Warre was perfectly competent as both a debater and a persuader. He had comfortably sat in the hallowed chambers of the English House of Lords—an ominous, overpowering setting if ever there was one!—and had never been the least bit intimidated by either those majestic surroundings, nor his eloquent, feisty colleagues. He had quite easily weathered the provocations and tauntings which greeted him when his own son was implicated in the attempted coup of 1601 led by the Earl of Essex. Such a crisis had not had the slightest impact on either his confidence or his oratory skills. Therefore, standing on the picturesque, wooded banks of Chesapeake Bay, although these surroundings were quite unfamiliar to him, this erstwhile Lord was confidently at ease.

He listened to various viewpoints and counter-arguments and eventually gained full approval to try it for just one more year. If the odds still proved to be overwhelmingly too great, then he indicated that he would be quite willing to arrange for repatriation for those who remained dis-satisfied. For his own part, he announced that he was preparing a full report to be dispatched forthwith to London, furnishing the Virginia Company's officers with all details regarding the state of affairs in the tenuously-balanced colony. He would carefully list the requirements and recommendations which had been submitted to the Council—and even include their suggestions with regards to which seeds might be needed for the upcoming crop-plantings.

He also learnt, for the first time, the full details which had plagued the relief fleet of 1609, and listened with total fascination to the remarkable story told by the passengers and crew of the ill-fated "Sea Venture." They had, he informed them, all been reported missing and presumed dead. Word of their fate had reached England previously when Captain John Smith was obliged to return from Jamestown following a serious accident to his leg and abdomen. Having had the chance to talk with the officers and crew of the boats which had limped to safety that year, Smith had justifiably agreed with them that little hope should be held for ever seeing Sir George Somers and his party again.

Sir George had by now already completed his own account of the shipwreck and Bermuda; it was all contained in a letter addressed to Robert Cecil, the Earl of Salisbury and Lord Treasurer of England. His report was brief and precise, a diplomatic gesture of respect to the kind offices of The Crown, whose ultimate authority had granted approval and encouragement for the relief fleet to finally leave Plymouth. With de la Warre, Somers spoke very highly of the islands where they had been forced to live for the last ten months. He talked enthusiastically and favourably, as if eager to dispel once and for all the wrong impressions of The Bermudas which the Spanish had given when they referred to them as "Los Diablos." On the contrary, Sir George regarded them as "Paradise."

Simultaneously, Silvester Jordain and William Strachey were putting the final touches to their own private recollections and explanations of the events of the last year. Perhaps above all others, their words would especially fire the imaginations of playwrights and historians for centuries to come.

Having at least come to terms with the overall future of the Virginia colony, the Council then turned straightaway to face the more immediate and pressing problems which plagued them. Foremost among these was the matter of a critical shortage of general provisions, especially fresh food.

On 13th. June, the second full day of the Council's deliberations, Sir George Somers rose to address the meeting. Wearing a long cloak and a bodice with padded epaulets, he struck an impressive figure. His shoulders were quite broad, his arms strong and muscular from performing the chores of a seaman; his hands and face were creased and cracked from continual exposure to the sun and driving waves. But he had aged in that last year and Lord de la Warre must have noticed this from the last time that they had met in London.

Sir George noted that his group of survivors had only recently left Bermuda, a place which they knew to have a most abundant quantity of fish, turtles and wild hogs. He heartily confirmed Strachy's claims about a profusion of wild birds with hundreds and hundreds of nests and eggs. In short, he remarked that he was quite willing to offer his services and return once more to those islands with his boat and crew. He maintained they would easily load "Patience" with plenty of food for the entire Jamestown community.

There appears to have been virtually no discussion of the offer; it was "thankfullie accepted." The gesture was magnanimous indeed, especially coming from one who had just arrived from that same desolate spot and continued to show signs of fatigue and concern; he was still tense from the responsibility which he had born all those months for the well-being of his crew and passengers. On 15th. June, he was officially charged with the duty of undertaking the return voyage.

Somers projected that it might take five weeks of travelling to and from Bermuda and probably another few weeks for collecting adequate provisions. He therefore anticipated that he would be gone for about eight weeks and tentatively set his return for the end of August, if not earlier. The Council proposed that for their part, the remainder should once again start to re-establish the abandoned settlement.

With these issues clearly and unanimously resolved, Somers designated his nephew Matthew Somers to prepare "Patience" once more for sea-worthiness. Whilst this was being done, it afforded the opportunity to snatch fragments of news about events which had occurred whilst they were all accepted as being "lost at sea."

On a personal level, Lord de la Warre could offer Sir George no particular words about his wife. Joane, clearly, had again had to sit through the anxieties and troubles which had typified her married life. Sir George knew that she would not readily despair and abandon all hope, but he must have felt frustration at not yet being able to assure her that he was still alive and well. It was some consolation, however, that he could now expect to be back at Berne Manor by Christmas. He also learnt that King James had handed Sherbourne Manor into the trusteeship of Robert Carr, the Earl of Somerset; this had formerly been the property of Sir Walter Raleigh, still in prison, and the transfer of ownership doubtless plucked a sentimental chord in Sir George's heart. Poor Raleigh!

As a navigator, Somers was astounded to learn that the eminent Italian astronomer Galileo Galilei (1564-1642) had now used his telescope to confirm that the moon's surface was not smooth, as usually presumed, but pocked with what appeared to be volcanic craters. He had followed such scientific advances with awe, as had other mariners, appreciating that with the development of the telescope in 1608 by Jensen and Metius the heavens would never be the same again. De la Warre might also have passed-on the rumour that Galileo was further claiming to have observed peculiar spots on the face of the sun . . . but then such fanciful tales always followed in the wake of new inventions!

On the political scene of Europe, there was the news that the Duke of Bavaria had formed the Catholic League—a fact which indicated the continuing rise of the Pope's policy to impose his religious views throughout the entire continent; such a move also served to further unite the independent states of the Hapsburg Empire into one single entity. Of casual interest was the news that King Philip III of Spain had another heir, a baby boy born in 1609 and named Ferdinand. None of them yet knew that on 14th. May, the King of France had been assassinated by a fanatic.

Then too there was the gossip of the Court of King James himself, of interest to enliven even the most depressing situations! Around a glowing fire by the waters of Chesapeake Bay, we can imagine the officers chuckling at the antics of the wayward Earl of Southampton, Henry Wriothesley. That year he had dropped even deeper into the habits of drinking and brawling and Somers' party must have been amused to hear of his latest antic—in which he had hit the Earl of Montgomery over the head with a tennis racquet during the course of a gentlemanly game. The King, according to eyewitnesses, had actually had to step in and separate the battling duo! And there was also the story of the King's cousin Arabella Stuart who everyone was evidently expecting to marry William Seymour—her longtime lover—in open defiance of the King's own personal orders. That would be a scandal indeed!

In 1610, Sir George's nephew Nicholas had just been appointed Master of the vessel "Christopher." It was a piece of information which pleased him considerably.

On June 19th. "Patience" was finally declared ready and they set sail. It is hard to imagine the courage of men such as these, casting-off into the open ocean in a completely home-made vessel when they might just as easily have borrowed one of the more rigid vessels of de la Warre's fleet. But this was their confidence, their gesture of faith in themselves and their skills. Accompanying them was a second boat, "Discovery" under Captain Samuel Argylle. If Somers' claims were as true as he had maintained, then it was felt that the more food he could provide so the better would be the chances of the colonists surviving the winter ahead.

In the interim, Captain Robert Tyndall was ordered to fish the waters between the twin capes of Cape Henry and Cape Charles, and return as soon as he had sufficient fish for the immediate weeks ahead. Tyndall had already left on 17th. June and was sighted by Sir George's party as they glided up the inlet towards the Atlantic. Mercifully, the success of Tyndall's group was considerably greater than that of another party which had been dispatched to trade for food among the Indians. The crew of "Swallow"—one of the original 1609 boats—had secured vast quantities of corn and then promptly mutinied! They stole the food and the boat, and became pirates!

On 22nd. June, as soon as "Patience" and "Discovery" were beyond the protection of the bay, they soon fell into the most violent of storms; giant waves washed the decks and wantonly pitched both boats from crest to trough. Pilots and navigators alike struggled to keep their course, whilst the drenched and jostled deckhands tugged at ropes and fought the customary battle between wind and canvas sails. As Somers and Argylle shouted their respective orders, they steadily drifted far to the north of their intended chart plan, closer to Cape Cod. And as they did so, each began to realise that the two boats were drawing further and further apart. By June 24th. they had lost sight of one another. They would never meet again.

Argylle soon surrendered to the whims of the elements and headed northwards, and then north-by-north-west until he again sighted land. In the sheltered calm of the shore, he turned southwards and eventually returned to Jamestown. We may but speculate about the reception which greeted his horrifying news that Sir George Somers was last seen heading out into the Atlantic Ocean once again being severely battered by a storm. Could it be, they may have wondered, that this time he would not return? It was a formidable re-run of similar reports which the remnants of his fleet had delivered to Virginia barely a year earlier. "Sir George Somers was last seen being battered by a severe tempest . . ." Once more, those on land would have to await the unknown. Maybe his reputation as a seaman, navigator and survivor were sufficient to allay immediate worries.

In any event, the storm dissipated; the winds dropped and the waters around the small pinnace became calm. The fragile "Patience" again provided remarkable testimony as to the skills of her builders. Sir George resumed his original tack and headed south-east, into the Gulf Stream and towards Bermuda.

If de la Warre's party were surprised to see Captain Argylle returning alone, then equally as startled must have been the reaction of Christopher Carter and Robert Waters at the beginning of July. There, approaching from the south-south-east they caught a glimpse of a boat heading toward them. And as it got closer they realised that it was "Patience," returning. But why? Had they never reached Virginia at all? What could they expect to find on board after well over a month at sea? The questions must have raced through their minds in rapid succession as they stood atop that pinnacle known as "Strachey's Watch," and stared at the vessel as it followed the reefs, passed through those shoals called "Somers Creek" and then dropped anchor.

Sir George Somers, his crew and the two islanders were jubilant at being together again, albeit rather unexpectedly so soon. There was relief also to know the reason for their hasty return and the urgent nature of their mission. Excitement filled the air at this welcome reunion, and they sat together on the beach to exchange notes on respective activities and occurrences during the previous two months.

Whereas everything which we know about Sir George Somers leads to the inevitable conclusion that his return to Bermuda was for no other reason than to provide honourable and responsible help to Jamestown, it is appropriate to pause here for a moment and explore another prevalent line of thought.

In the British Museum there is an unidentified manuscript of some 363 pages of handwritten text. It is generally accepted that this document is the work of either Captain John Smith or Governor Nathaniel Butler, possibly edited or checked by Dr. William Creshaw—the same gentleman who furnished the preface for Silvester Jourdain's report. The argument proposed by this document is partially at odds with the accepted viewpoint and suggests some other, slightly more selfish motive as lying behind the enthusiastic return which Sir George so readily made to Bermuda.

Smith, or whomever is the author, suggests that prior to leaving, Sir George had promised Carter and Waters that he would return as soon as possible because he was eager for an excuse to have another thorough look at the islands with an eye to a future business venture. Although they had all been stranded on Bermuda for ten long months, so pre-occupied had they been with the building of escape boats and simply surviving, that only the scantiest of opportunities had been presented for a detailed exploration of the various islands. Somers had made a crude map, but that was about all that he had managed. Therefore, he directed Carter and Waters to undertake a detailed exploration of each island and to try to shed "light of the commodities of the soil" so that they might be able to prepare a report on the potential of a future plantation development. According to this manuscript, Somers returned primarily in order to get an up-date report prior to eventually leaving Virginia for England later that year.

It is certainly uncharitable to the memory of Sir George Somers and his loyal crew to believe that such was the sole and self-serving motive which caused him to return to Bermuda a second time. Actually, all of the evidence and testimony of contemporaries does nothing more than verify that they returned to acquire food for the Jamestown settlers. We know that he was enchanted by the thought of developing Bermuda and had placed it high on his list of priorities for when he was back in England. Probably he did set Carter and Waters the task of undertaking a complete survey of the area's potential; but he **had** prepared them for a two year gap between his initial departure and the anticipated date of return. If he took some advantage of an unexpectedly speedy return, then so be it; but this was hardly his prime motive for setting-out from Chesapeake on June 19th.

In the words of Lord de la Warre: ". . . this good old gentleman, out of his love and zeal, most cheerfully and resolutely undertook to perform this dangerous voyage."

During July and August, the sailors hunted and fished with great determination and vigour. They set about their tasks rapidly and eagerly. Each had a definite and solitary goal: to load "Patience" with as much fish and meat as possible, deliver it to Virginia, and then return to their homes in the towns and villages of south-west England. Their thoughts had now turned very much to families, friends, children, wives; their job took them to sea, but they were homely nevertheless.

Something now, however, began to happen. The hurricane season was underway and there were often days when the seas were far too rough to enable them to fish off-shore. Sometimes the winds blew dangerously and they chose not to chase wild hog at distances increasingly further and further away from camp.

Many of the young chicks had hatched and so there were not so many eggs for them to pluck from the more accessible parts of the cliffs. Their labours slowed; weeks slipped by. "Patience" was still not full.

Furthermore, it had now become apparent that Sir George himself was unwell. At first it was concluded by Matthew that his uncle was probably suffering the delayed effects of the strains and anguish of the previous twelve months; he expected that with some rest and relaxation he would soon be his normal self again. Then they would get back into the full stride of hunting and fishing and be off once more. But his was not to be. September turned into October and Sir George Somers was clearly continuing to deteriorate.

At a distance of nearly four centuries and with neither a body nor any autopsy report, it is very difficult to diagnose the precise nature of his illness. But we may logically reconstruct the circumstances.

There is absolutely no doubt at all that by the time that he reached Virginia he was physically and mentally exhausted. As Admiral of the Fleet, charged with the dual responsibilities of transporting new settlers and also providing urgently-required relief to the Jamestown colonists, his burden was indeed great. The shipwrecking of the "Sea Venture," however, compounded his efforts and resulted in his having to shoulder some truly enormous worries. He was worried because he might very well have lost his entire fleet, and didn't know for sure; he was worried because he was charged with the responsibility of saving an entire colony, and had perhaps now caused its total loss of life. He was worried for the well-being of those who had survived with him and whose lives he now had to carry to safety. He was worried about being unable to inform his wife and the Company in London that **his** party, at least, was still safe.

As a professional man, Sir George probably revealed none of these worries to anyone; rather they were kept inside, evolving into a knot of internal nervous disorders. By the time that he reached Virginia, he was already critically run-down. His nervous system was in a state of extreme distress; his metabolic balance was awry. It was in this weakened condition that he chose to push himself even further, by volunteering to return to Bermuda without allowing the opportunity to at least physically recuperate. It was a gesture which pushed his reserves to breaking-point.

By the time that "Patience" was again at anchor in the clear Bermudian waters, Sir George Somers was seriously ill. The relentless pressures and worries of the preceeding months had now begun to manifest themselves as gastric disorders; it is possible that he had the early beginnings of an ulcer. However, of far graver consequence, one medical opinion now suggests that it seems highly probable that he was suffering from a bout of hepatitis. This is a debilitating complaint frequently born of unhygenic conditions, which not only produces increasing listlessness and fatigue but which also reduces the liver's ability to produce sufficient anti-bodies to counteract the disease-producing poisons (toxins) of bacteria.

Aware of his continuing physical collapse, he prepared Matthew for the likelihood that he would not live to return to Virginia. He therefore instructed that once the boat was adequately stocked with provisions they should return forthwith and fulfill his commitment to Lord de la Warre and the beleaguered colonists of Jamestown. He then directed that Matthew should make haste for England and assemble sufficient financial backing to fund a proper expedition to Bermuda. It was something which he had intended to do himself as soon as he got back, seeking to develop these islands "by the purse and means of himself and his friends."

In documents of the sixteenth and seventeenth centuries, there were certain stock phrases to explain the sicknesses which befell seamen. They tended to have "a sudden fever," or "a sweating sickness." Others got "dystemper" or, as was the case of 60 men who died in Hispaniola, they suffered from "a flux of the bellie." But nowhere do we find references to feverish conditions. Rather, Sir George Somers health was classified as "a gradual decay" which chronicler John Stowe attributed to "a surfeit of pig."

The inevitable conclusion from the evidence is that somewhere towards late October his deteriorating condition was finally assaulted by food-poisoning. (The bacteria **staphylococcus**, in particular, grows rampantly in warmer conditions and food cured in salt is a particularly good medium for its growth. Patients rarely die from it now—but things were different then.) Already in poorer health than the others in his party, Sir George's body was especially susceptible to such a sickness—an illness which was not reported as widespread among the others of his crew.

Almost daily, the mood in the small encampment became gloomier as each man came to accept within himself that this "Worthie sailor" whom they had come to admire and respect, was gradually and irreversibly growing weaker and weaker. He was often prostrate, he vomitted and lingered in a state of shock.

Their efforts came to a virtual standstill. Fish were caught and eaten; water was collected and they drank it. As their beloved Admiral visibly deteriorated, so they became drained of any clear purpose. October had ended and another month idled into view.

Then, in the words of John Smith, "when labouring with these desires, it pleased God to ease them of him . . . by taking him out of this world . . ."

It was Friday November 9th. 1610. Sir George Somers was dead.

Chesapeake Bay Area—after White—1590.

Courtesy of State Department of Archives and History.

17

Back To England For Burial

The dust of reality was slow to settle but when it did, and they realised that they were in effect stranded without their leader, this unexpected dilemma was emotionally and lustily debated. Matthew Somers, of course, was still the Captain of "Patience" and heir apparent to the mantle of total leadership; but he lacked the natural qualities of authority and charisma which had been so characteristic of his noble uncle. As discussions seemingly became more heated, Matthew was forced to remind his men of Sir George's last instruction—that they must first return to Virginia and fulfill their obligations to those who still stood on the shores of Chesapeake Bay awaiting their arrival. But reason had ceased to be a major factor in their deliberations.

Opinions had split unevenly into two opposing directions. There were those who felt a totally loyal and blind commitment towards carrying-out the final order of Sir George; they wanted to head for Virginia without further delay. But they had already more than adequately endured and proven themselves for The Company and Jamestown alike. It was argued that surely after the five month delay since they had slipped passed Cape Henry, the colonists had come to accept Captain Argylle's assumption that "Patience" and her crew were lost at sea. With the North American winter firmly taking a grip on their daily lives, it was argued that surely no-one was still hoping that they would afterall reappear over the horizon. Jamestown **must** have made alternative plans? It was inconceivable that Lord de la Warre was still sitting idly on the shoreline awaiting the return of a boat which might well have long-since sunk!

And so it was that the initial divisiveness of Matthew Somers' band of sailors became a single-minded plan to sail directly for England.

But the untimely death of Sir George Somers had provided those aboard "Patience" with a complex network of dilemmas, each of which placed the men in a very serious predicament.

Due to the irregular circumstances which had precipitated their mercy mission to Bermuda, the boat was manned by a hastily assembled group of general volunteers, most of whom were personally devoted to Admiral Somers. It was not a finely balanced team, but rather a spontaneous mixture of mariners put together for just this single, supposedly brief voyage. Due to the relatively safe nature of the passage to Bermuda, they had not felt it necessary to carry a ship's doctor—such professionals were of greater value tending to the decimated townsfolk of Jamestown. Now, they had a predicament which was real indeed: before them lay the body of Sir George Somers, an English Admiral commissioned to his rank with the approval of King James—and none of them was competent to explain precisely why he had died!

In those days of vagabonds and mutinies, such medical ignorance could actually have proved to be weighty indeed. It was further compounded by the fact that not only did they have the death of an eminent Elizabethan seaman to try to explain, but also they would have to account for their decision to defy the orders of Lord de la Warre **and** Sir George Somers, by neglecting Virginia and returning to England. The days immediately following his death unquestionably became woven into a very serious pattern of problems.

In his account of the aftermath of Sir George's death, Captain John Smith in "History of Virginia" notes that the body was secretly stowed aboard the boat; that his heart was cut-out and buried in the ground of the islands which he had come to know and love so dearly. With these two things accomplished, they purportedly casted-off and headed for England.

Smith wrote the bulk of this material in about 1619; he had, of course, never been to Bermuda personally and his fame as a writer rests primarily on his genuine interest in the subjects about which he wrote. He was an editor and compiler, a presenter of the narratives of others. In fact, reacting to his own efforts to record these events as part of Virginia's early history, he frequently lamented the fact that all he ever got in return was abuse! In light of this, we might perhaps look a little more closely at his summary of what he says occurred with regards to the removal of Sir George's heart and the stowing-away of his body.

There is not much doubt that a body was finally carried to England. Sinister mutterings abound even to this day that Matthew Somers needed an actual body to verify his uncle's death, purely in order that he might prove that he **was** dead and thus come into the benefits of the will. Whether this is truly what his motives were is arguable. With an entire crew to testify that Sir George was dead, it is difficult to see that a body would have been required—especially when it was not usual to take dead bodies back home for burial . . . and dying was cleary an occupational hazzard for these adventurers!

No, it is far more likely that they opted to take the body back with them as some rather naive proof that he had not actually been killed or otherwise mysteriously disposed of. They already anticipated having to answer a serious barrage of questions about defying explicit orders to return to Virginia. At least having the body to present might clear them of any wrong-doing with regards to that! It was an irregular thing to do, highly abnormal conduct without much conventional precedence. If we choose to dismiss the oft-quoted and self-serving motives of Matthew Somers, then at least this proposition still stands as plausible.

What is highly questionable, however, is Smith's allegation that the body was stowed-away, "carried to England secretly in a cedar chest" and put aboard the ship in such a manner as to have totally deceived the crew as to what was really in the box. But this is quite difficult to imagine, particularly when placed into the purely practical sequence of acts involved. First of all, a funeral would have had to have been faked—remarkably hard to accomplish effectively among such a small group. And if there had been no burial, then there would have been endless questions with regards to the disposal of the body . . . these were highly superstitious times and bodies just simply didn't vanish; nor were they casually forgotten. Secondly, it is very hard to imagine that the majority of the ship's compliment did not notice the cumbersome box going aboard "Patience." A makeshift coffin is awkward to carry; this one had to be ferried by rowing boat out to a ship at anchor, and then hauled up over the rails and placed somewhere on deck. Other provisions were being regularily taken out and then salted in barrels; do we have to imagine that none of the sailors noticed that this particular cumbersome commodity was receiving special respect?

Without doubt, the crew had to overcome personal worries about carrying a dead body. It rather went against their own traditional superstitions because, as Smith correctly observes, they held "the portage of dead bodies extremely, prodigiously ominous." These were the days when seafaring superstitions were reaching a peak; in the era of extraordinary discoveries and explorations, mariners consistently went to new places and saw hitherto unknown animals, plants, trees and people. Long journeys exposed them to previously unknown natural phenomenon. It was the time when tales were spread to explain the disappearances of ships, dragged to the depths by the tentacles of some serpent or giant squid. Their maps were beautifully illustrated with monsters and water-squirting fish of gigantic proportions. And deeply-religious backgrounds had firmly implanted precise ideas about spirits and the departing souls of the dead.

They surely **did** know that they were carrying the body of Sir George Somers back to England. Their motive for doing so was clearly sufficiently important for them to shun instinctive worries and take it with them.

Some preservation of the corpse was inevitably undertaken. It was a basic and primitive embalming, consisting of the removal of the entrails and vital organs, followed by treating the body with a salt solution. All of this offal was then duly buried in accordance with Sir George's expressed wish to have his heart left in Bermuda. (Cutting-out and burying a heart was not at all unusual in those days. The family of Queen Anne Boleyn stored hers for many years; whilst the descendents of Henry Grey and, later, Sir Walter Raleigh, reputedly kept the actual heads of their loved ones!) What happened to that bloody package is another issue altogether.

Bermudian tradition indicates that his heart lies buried in a tomb in the aptly-named "Somers Gardens," in the old Capital of St. George. But there is no solid proof as to its precise and original location. In 1620, Governor Butler reputedly came across a wooden marker in the undergrowth which an aide told him was the original wooden cross used to mark the spot where the heart was buried. Some time later, that same Governor arranged for the erection of a more permanent slab of marble to replace the cross. A brass plaque was subsequently implanted on the monument—although somehow the entire monument was "lost" after about 1675.

In 1819, the actual tomb customarily held to contain the heart and entrails of Sir George Somers was officially opened by Admiral Sir David Milne. Amidst considerable apprehension and drama, the opened shrine was exposed to contain only a few fragments of glass; however no serious or scientific examination of these important contents was ever made. Alas! The date of the vessel will now never be known, nor shall we ever have the chance to scrutinise any traces of what had formerly been within it. Regrettably, this vital information is lost forever.

In 1882, Governor Sir J. Henry Lefroy presented a volume of Bermudian history to the prestigious Hakluyt Society of London, and he firmly concluded that the tomb probably was somewhere near to the actual site where the heart was first buried. Under his direction, a memorial was erected in 1876 and he again reiterated his conviction that it is "near this spot . . ." that the original heart was interred.

And so it was that towards the middle of November 1610, Matthew Somers and the men from "Patience" concluded their deliberations and set their plans into action. The body of Sir George Somers was crudely embalmed; his heart and entrails were buried on the southern side of contemporary St. George's Island. A small creek extended inland from what is now The Town Square and wound its way along the modern-day road which is in front of Somers Gardens. By choosing this spot as the place to leave the Admiral's heart, they were therefore placing it in a protected area by the water. It was a location which they had obviously given thought to.

After this, they set about the task of supplementing the provisions which they had been gathering prior to Sir George's death and then they were ready to leave.

With due consideration to the dying orders imposed upon Matthew—that he should hastily prepare a full Bermuda expedition from England—Christopher Carter and Robert Waters agreed to remain, in accordance to their original agreement with Sir George. Subsequent accounts suggest that Carter had opted to stay in Bermuda alone, evidently confident that nephew Matthew would be able to organise a return trip for the following year. In a series of last-minute decisions it was decided that Waters should remain behind with Carter, along with one belated volunteer in the form of Edward Charde. There is little reason to dispute the popular belief that these three willingly chose to remain, at least in part, out of genuine loyalty to the Bermuda aspiration of Admiral Somers—a man whom each had come to hold in the highest regard.

Oddly enough, there is no verifiable source to provide the exact date of when they eventually departed. It is most likely to have been in the late Spring of 1611, a time when wintery squalls and rough seas have invariably given way to more pleasant waters in this part of the Atlantic Ocean. Having been shipwrecked in 1609, and then severely battered by another storm in 1610, they could scarcely have been blamed for cautiously denying credence to the possibility of this being their "third time lucky!"

Allowing for between six to eight weeks for the crossing, we may estimate that "Patience" headed through the eastern reefs towards the end of March or early April 1611. Carter, Charde and Waters watched it gently blowing towards the horizon; its sails fully-stretched and straining. It was an emotional moment, a sombre ending to a truly astounding voyage—the details of which none of them could have predicted in even the most bizarre of dreams during the days before they had left Plymouth, close to two years before.

"Patience" carefully slipped free of the reef and veered to the north. They chose to take the northerly route back to England, one which would eventually merge them with the shipping lanes used by fishing boats and one with which they were more familiar. There had never been a specific route from Bermuda to England as such, although when travelling from the West Indies it was conventional to head towards these islands and then continue northwards to the Grand Banks, before then turning eastward to England. Without allowing for wind-tacks, the distance arced itself through roughly two thousand miles of open water. Having taken nearly eleven days for this same boat to reach Virginia, Matthew Somers calculated that at a similarily plodding speed of about 55 miles per day they would be lucky to reach their destination within two months. It would be a slow, tiring journey.

The townsfolk of Lyme Regis, of course, were still totally unaware of the fate of "Patience" and its crew. Lord de la Warre had conveyed the pessimistic opinion of Captain Argylle—who had been the very last person to actually see the boat ten months earlier. For a second time, there was every indication that the ship's crew had all been drowned. Sadly, yet realistically, they had come to accept that none of their menfolk would return, although within each heart there was probably a lingering hope, that final wish that somehow a miracle had preserved them once more.

No-one, therefore, was prepared for the curious sight which

came into view off The Cobb on or about June 1st. 1611. Through the morning mists of the English Channel, they noticed the forlorn approach of a distinctly weather-beaten pinnace. There was something not quite conventional about its lines and design; it was a boat which none of them had seen before. Gradually it glided closer into the shore, becoming quite apparent that it intended to dock against The Cobb. Then, as it got closer and closer, the people began to hear familiar voices and recognise faces, eyes and even waves and smiles. For many of the people of Lyme Regis that day, the true miracle had really come in answer to their prayers. The atmosphere must have spontaneously erupted into uncontrollable joy as word of the mystery boat fled excitedly throughout the homes and shops from Broad Street right up to the end of Coombe Street.

Just as immediate, however, would have passed the tragic news about the body of Sir George Somers. That he alone was dead must have been a deeply-felt tragedy. It was hard for them to grasp that their most famous son had died.

John Somers was summonsed down to The Cobb fairly quickly. Matthew's mother and his wife (the former Joan Roope) came shortly afterwards, accompanied by his brother Nicholas. For the Somers family it was an occasion of mixed grief and joy. As the nominal head of the family, it was also John's responsibility to quickly arrange for someone to ride directly out to Berne Manor and appraise Lady Somers of the freshly-unveiled and tragic events. There is no record of who was sent on that unsought errand. John had to remain and take charge of the body in Lyme itself; he presumably sent a close family friend to break the news to the widow—or "relict", in the term of those days.

On the surface, it is surprising to learn that there are no lengthy descriptions in the Lyme Regis or Dorset archives relating to the death of Sir George Somers. There was no period of official mourning; no form of lying-in-state; not even a reference to it in the minutes of the local council meetings. On the other hand, this may not be strange at all when we consider that during the previous twenty-four months Sir George had been accepted as dead on at least two separate occasions. He was, at that very moment, still assumed to have been long-since dead. The totally unexpected arrival of a boat carrying his body was far beyond anyone's expectations, or comprehension. No official reception, nor special treatment in any form whatsoever, could have been undertaken.

From all available evidence, the arrangements were mainly for family.

Following seafaring custom, the dead body was taken ashore first, accompanied by a short volley fired by a hastily-assembled row of musketmen. The boat had been tied fast at the far end of The Cobb and so the cedar box which contained his remains was carefully brought up the narrow steps on that inner edge, and then rested on the flat surface of the sea-wall. Nearby fluttered the English flag, hoisted up that same flagpole which young George had gazed at so often as a child. The adjacent cannon fired a single shot, sufficient to pay respect to a fallen soldier without causing undue alarm within the neighbouring villages.

Sir George's widow is unlikely to have arrived in Lyme until the following day. Although she had long been accustomed to the uncertainties of being married to a merchant-adventurer, she still needed some private moments to adjust to the undeniable fact that her husband was no longer merely "presumed" to be dead. She also needed time to make preliminary steps to arrange for a funeral at their local church in Whitchurch Canonicorum. The next morning, after attending regular service, she made her sad way into Lyme Regis in order to claim the body of her husband.

Identification was really unnecessary, since a bona fide member of the family had been present at the time of death and could testify that he and the entire crew knew it to be the body of Sir George Somers. His brother John may have chosen to make a brief inspection, but by this time the remains were in a state of advanced decomposition. Joane Somers is not likely to have looked at her husband's corpse at all; it is never pleasant to look death in the face. It would have been pointless for her to glance at the corpse of a loved one who had already been dead for close to eight months. There was no point in her confirming for herself what she already knew to be true. The sad procession returned to Berne Manor that same day.

John Somers remained in Lyme Regis. He had to take legal custody of the will the following day, a Monday. After this, he would then join them at Berne for a burial which they anticipated would take place on the Tuesday.

The roads which Joane Somers took her sad carriage along were the same ones which Sir George had taken himself on that last day when he had waved his farewells. They were the same bumpy "weyes," narrow and overgrown with trees and bushes. In places, the cedar chest bounced and banged in the back of the wagon; at times a single horse was obliged to step towards the undergrowth in order to let them pass. They headed into Charmouth and then out the other side. Along the roadways, people stopped to watch them go by for the news about their dark cargo had become commonplace throughout Dorset within hours of "Patience" arrival the previous day.

On Monday morning, June 3rd. 1611, John Somers entered the Lyme Regis town hall and officially claimed a box deposited there on the instructions of Sir George Somers. It was to be collected by his brother in the event of his death. The box was duly handed over and the contents verified by the assembled Council members. He left for Berne.

The funeral for Sir George Somers took place on Tuesday June 4th., in the small church of St. Wita's (St. Candida and Holy Cross), Whitchurch Canonicorum. The distance from Berne Manor to the church is quite short and should not have taken them much more than fifteen or so minutes.

It is a small church, but has an impressive history dating back into Saxon times, with ties closely linking it to King Alfred the Great and even William the Conqueror. The procession of mourners passed through the small cluster of homes which constitute the hamlet of Whitchurch and then paused briefly at the tall cross outside the entrance to the grounds. The name of St. Candida was merely the Latin version of St. Wita, the original Anglo-Saxon name for the saint whose remains rested within a shrine inside the church. The bones were contained within a stone coffin beneath the north window and were of such importance that they attracted pilgrims from all parts of the country to pay homage. Such famous company for the body they were preparing to bring for burial must have crossed through the minds of the Somers family.

They passed beyond the main gates and followed the short pathway which curves gently through various marble and granite headstones in the surrounding cemetery. They shuffled and dragged their feet under the weight of the coffin. There is no record of who the pall-bearers were, but they may well have included Baldwin Sanford and possibly Matthew Somers. John Somers followed closely behind the casket, supporting his own wife and his grieving sister-in-law.

The great wooden door in the porch was already opened, so that they walked through the shadows and emerged directly at the head of the nave. To one side stood the font which Joane and George Somers had hoped would one day bear witness to the baptism of their own children. But this had never been. Either side of the aisle there rose smooth columns, each topped by a hand-carved stone capital dating back into the twelfth century.

Elegant Norman arches rose over the windows, pointing upwards at the intricate vaulting of the roof.

The funeral party quietly stepped over the stone flooring, each sensing not only the solemnity of their own private occasion, but also sensitive to the sober aurora which pervaded the church itself. There is still something in the chilly atmosphere which evokes an awareness of Saints and people from much earlier centuries.

It was a short service, more of a memorial than a conventional funeral. There was no lamenting over recently-departed souls; they had come to finally bury the remains of a man who had died the previous year; his spirit had presumably long-since departed into heaven. They now only sought blessings for his physical body, the ultimate act of grace which they could offer his memory before committing him to the ground.

In the north wall of the chancel the mourners noticed the preparations which were being made for an elaborate tomb, complete with the recumbent effigy of a nobleman; Sir John Jeffrey, the owner of Catherston Manor had just died that previous May 7th. and his sculptured memorial was not yet complete. Arrangements had been made for the body of Sir George Somers to be buried beneath the floor of the nearby chantry (now the vestry), an area endowed by Henry de Greneford in the thirteenth century. It was a prominent place within the church, one favoured by the family and the resident clergy as being appropriate to the high esteem which they all held for this remarkable man.

After the closing words, chief mourners left and returned to Berne Manor. And at some time later that same night, the heavy stones in the floor of the chantry were raised and the body of Sir George Somers was steadily lowered into its final resting place.

* * * * * *

There is one final postscript to the curious death and burial of Sir George Somers. In a letter dated August 2nd. 1984, an authority at the church in Whitchurch Canonicorum remarks that:

> ". . . Sir George's body was not placed under the chancel, but under the original chantry now the vestry. This has been fully inspected not only by me and my predecessors, but also by a television team searching for history in the South West. There are tomb stones but they do not refer to Sir George. One must assume that no

record was left."

More ominously, the correspondent remarks:

"I have no original documentation about the date of his burial and cannot confirm that he was actually buried."

18

The Last Will
And Testament

In the life of Sir George Somers there remained little else but to read the will and distribute his estate in accordance with his final wishes.

The deceased had been a careful, meticulous man when alive and his will reflected these traits.

It had been written in the last days before he left Berne Manor for the trip to Virginia. It is dated 23rd. April 1609, St. George's Day. He had clearly spend a great deal of time and thought on its preparation, and was equally as precise about where it should be stored, by whom it should be read, and which witnesses were to be present at the reading. He had wanted no ambiguities, no doubts over his last requests.

The document was sealed in a solid wooden box and entrusted to the office of the Mayor of Lyme Regis, complete with instructions as to who should collect it in the event of his death, and who should also be in attendance to authenticate the nature of the contents. Everything seemed to be clearly arranged, as if he had a premonition about his pending fate.

He was also remarkably cautious, almost suspicious lest anything be tampered with before its time. A story even abounds that after he had completed the will and locked it in the box, he would frequently go back into the house and check that it was still untouched—perhaps he was suspicious that even his own wife might be eager for a sneak preview!

June 3rd. 1610 was a Monday and a small solemn group of men had gathered in the office of Mr. James Hill, the Mayor of Lyme Regis. At their customary places in the chamber sat the other members of the town Corporation: Mr. John Hazzard, Junior; Mr. Richard Norris; Mr. Walter Tucker; Mr. Robert Brag; Mr. John Theridge and Mr. Richard Carpenter. Each of the committee members was well-known to Sir George Somers, most had worked with him for years on the town's governing body; they knew him as a former Mayor, as a Freeman of Lyme Regis and as a friend with whom they had grown-up.

But this was not a time for them to be drawn into their own private reflections and all eyes were turned to John Somers, brother of the deceased. With him stood James Seaward, Richard Hodg and Sir George's long-time tenant, advisor and friend Baldwyne Sanford. In accordance with the implicit instructions, John Somers formally requested the box which had been entrusted to the Mayor by the dead man; in his turn, James Hill handed it over, making sure that all present might bear witness to its pristine condition, confirming that it had not been tampered with. Then John Somers departed for Berne Manor.

After the funeral the family returned to the house for the reading of the will. John Somers placed a key in the lock, turned it and opened the lid. An air of apprehension filled the room, partly in response to the drama of the carefully orchestrated actions of those involved. He reached inside, removed the document and gently unfolded it.

After quickly scanning the sheet, John Somers then turned to those assembled and solemnly read aloud the last will and testament of Sir George Somers:

> "Intending to pass the seas in a voyage towards the land called Virginia," it began, "I bequeath to the poor of Whitechurch, co. Dorset, 20 pounds; to the poor of Lyme Regis, 10 pounds."

It was appropriate that a man who had come from almost nothing should first of all remember those who were far less fortunate than himself. It set the tone for the will and helped to establish a sense of kindness and benevolence. It perpetuated an image.

There then followed a list of financial bequests to be granted to the children of John Somers. William and John Junior were to each receive 100 pounds within the next two years; brother Toby and his sister Mary were to get the same amount each, as soon as they reached the age of twenty-one. Next it was announced that longtime household servant George Bird had been granted 20 pounds, as had Mr. Baldwyne Sanford.

The will then proceeds to give specific instructions with regards to the children of his deceased brother Nicholas. The eldest of his two sons, also called Nicholas, was to be granted the sum of 100 pounds, as well as full title to various tenements which Sir George had title to in Lyme Regis, and which were then being rented by one Robert Barnes. A condition was imposed on Nicholas, however, before he could claim his inheritence. In the first instance, all of this was to be held back until such time as Lady Somers herself had died. Secondly, it was dependent on Nicholas' formally withdrawing all future claims on Sir George's properties at Whitchurch, Marshwood and Upwaie (sic)—these were to go directly to his younger brother Matthew, once other conditions within the will had been discharged.

On the next line, John Somers was specifically designated as the executor of the will. He was charged with ensuring that any outstanding debts should be settled by using his properties at Whitchurch and Upwey, as well as a piece of land which he had recently acquired from a gentleman by the name of Richard Mallocke. Once more, it was plainly written that any monetary balance from those transactions must be passed over to his nephew Matthew.

Lady Somers was ensured of retaining Berne Manor, and any other of their holdings as still survived the settling of Sir George's debts, until she in turn passed away. An apparent exception, curiously enough, would appear to have been the contents of Berne itself, to which Matthew automatically became entitled to one-half. It must have been presumed that normal common decency would prevail and the eager seafaring nephew would at least wait until his aunt was dead, before he came to claim his half of the furnishings!

The will concluded by designating Baldwyne Sanford and James Heywood as the official overseers of the will. The latter was possibly Sir George's brother-in-law, intentionally appointed as a gesture of respect to his wife and her family. It was then signed by three imparting witnesses: Thomas Moleins, John Boylden and Henry Corbinne. None of these three was a beneficiary in the will. A final forethought by Sir George aimed at dispelling any question of coersion being exerted upon his final wishes.

The town clerk duly completed his official recording of the details relating to the reading of Sir George's will; then he made a comprehensive list of those who had been in attendance. The note was duly signed, validated and the gathering dispersed.

The details of the will quickly spread into the streets of Lyme Regis which were doubtless buzzing and humming with excitement for the remainder of the day. We can also presume that the somewhat over-weighted good fortunes of Matthew Somers, in particular, came in for a certain amount of questioning and gossip. So **that** was why Matthew had brought the Admiral's body back? So **that** was why he had broken tradition and carried a corpse nearly four thousand miles back across the Atlantic Ocean? So **that** was why he had effectively abandoned those in Virginia who were perhaps still awaiting their return from Bermuda with fresh meat? Matthew Somers' insistence on heading back to England, with a body to prove that Sir George was indeed dead, now began to assume a different complexion in the minds of the tongue-waggers of Dorset. There now appeared to be reason for why he had defied his uncle's last verbal request that they complete their mission and return to Virginia and the awaiting colonists.

But such is the making of gossip. It does nothing to take into account that Sir George's will had paid some dues to the poor, and had acknowledged the needs of the next generation of Somers children, as well as the continuing comforts of his faithful wife. Such idle tongues did nothing to acknowledge his clear-cut determination to settle all outstanding debts and to ensure that his wife was unburdened of the responsibilities of settling their far-flung affairs. He had thought of everything, knowing that he could trust his brother John to carry out these concluding wishes.

John Somers did indeed fulfill his obligations as executor of his deceased brother's will. Among the most impressive of the peripheral documents related to this, the full inventory of the contents of Berne Manor serves as a testimony to John Somers' dedication and responsibility. These two brothers had always been particularily close throughout their lives; John knew that this ultimate obligation would fall on his shoulders. He wanted to do it correctly and thoroughly, just as he knew George would expect it to be done. And so the inventory of Berne Manor, which John Somers formally laid before the Prerogative Court of Canterbury on 16th. August 1611—a remarkably prompt two months after the initial reading of the will—contains a complete listing of each and every item which Sir George and Lady Somers had gathered around themselves. Room-by-room, John Somers noted everything from sheets, to carpets, pillows, stools, chests and taffeta cloths. He lists bed covers; describes the andirons by the fireside, and even includes the curtains and cushions in the "chamber over the buttrie." Plates, pots and kettles are mentioned, alongside curtains, dishes, buckets, tables and cupboards.

Through the diligence of John Somers we are furnished with a detailed picture of the surroundings in which Sir George Somers passed the final years of his life. In sum total, we are given an image of a man nestled amidst the complete comforts of luxurious living. He provides us with a domestic scene in which nothing would seem to have been lacking—save the patter of their own children's feet. But even that was clearly compensated for by the diverse rewards which Sir George was able to assemble for them to use and enjoy—French tapestries, silks from the Orient, carpets from India and the delicate weavings of Damascus. He had the finest of everything which he owned.

In his last will and testament, Sir George Somers confirmed that he had indeed been a successful merchant adventurer, and a man who had grasped at the opportunities offered in Elizabethan England to people ambitious enough to meet the challenges of those exciting times. But he never lost touch with those around him, the poor people, his friends, a servant.

And it was also appropriate that he should bequeath the most to his younger descendents; that he should, in this way, pay homage to their hopes and dreams for the future. For even in death Sir George Somers remained a visionary. He had faith in what lay beyond the horizon.

19

On The Matter Of His Appearance

Throughout this present volume, an effort has been made to provide not only an historical survey of the life and times of Sir George Somers, but also to convey as much as possible about his character and personality.

We know that he was a respected leader, a man in whom the qualities of initiative and determination were cultivated from birth and developed throughout an entire life-time. We know too that he was a man raised to know and respect the sea and he became a seaman graced with a sharpness of mind to cope with her furious and fickle ways. Many years of navigating channels and oceans alike made Sir George Somers a decisive man, firm but well-liked by those who sailed as his crew.

Years of sea-faring tested his will and strength but, like his contemporaries, he had always stood full-square with pride at being a true Elizabethan seaman. Such men were confident, highly-motivated; they possessed a sense of purpose and worth and were held in high-esteem by those who caught glimpses of them in port.

But the endless chases through the Atlantic swells, and the battles in the waterways of the Caribbean and Europe inevitably took their toll. It showed not in weariness of spirit, but in the prematurely grey hair and deep furrows etched across the face. Thus by the time that Sir George Somers reached Bermuda, his appearance was unquestionably that of a weather-beaten sailor; his face and hands rouged and roughened by constant exposure to salty sprays and lashing seas. His face could have born none of the smoothness more characteristic of the courtiers and landed-gentry. Rather, creases must have marked the edges of his eyes and the corners of his mouth—as if frozen in an expression of permanent wincing and smarting, peering through fogs or blaring sunshine; forever on the look-out, always sensitive and alert to something unknown which might strike with terror from beyond the next wave.

And so, we are left with the final and nagging question: What did Sir George Somers actually look like?

History has bequeathed us only one apparently verified portrait of "this gallant knight." This is an oil painting attributed to the artist Paul Van Somers. It is currently owned by the Bermuda Historical Society and is on permanent display in the main library in Hamilton, the capital. It is a full-size picture, a companion to another which purports to show Lady Somers—the only known surviving likeness which we have of Sir George's wife. (Curiously enough, she is inexplicably identified as 'Winifred'!)

The Somers portraits had evidently been carefully preserved by successive members of the Bellamy family, a branch of proven direct-descendents of Sir George Somers who lived in Plymouth, England. The actual existence of the paintings seems not to have been widely known for several centuries, although they were part of the regular collection of exhibits displayed at the small Bellamy Museum in Plymouth.

In 1881, a black and white sketch had been made from the original oil painting by Lieutenant B. A. Branhill. This remains the prime illustration used in related articles and texts. But it was not until July 25th. 1908 that the actual portraits themselves were specifically publicised. On that day, during the course of a ceremony unveiling a commemorative brass plaque to Sir George Somers at Whitchurch Canonicorum, it was revealed that both pictures were to be restored with "possible mezzotinting."

This was presumably done, for they then received some degree of international exposure in 1929. Between April 29th. and May 25th. of that year, they were included in a special exhibition of portraits held in Virginia House, Richmond, Virginia, in the United States. The exhibition was held under the auspices of the Virginia Historical Society and was intended to feature a great range of individuals whose lives had touched on the history of the State of Virginia. The official programme for that event includes the whimper of a desire that the Somers portraits should stay in Virginia. But that was never to be. They have resided in Bermuda throughout much of this current century.

The painting of Sir George Somers shows a gentleman standing with his hand symbolically resting atop a small globe. In the upper left-hand side of the picture there is a three masted boat under full sail, suggesting the "Sea Venture." In the bottom right-hand corner there is unmistakably written "Sir George Somers."

Perhaps because the Van Somers original, and the subsequent Branhill print are the only known recorded likenesses of Sir George Somers, it is almost inevitable that the work should have generated a degree of controversy as to authenticity. The question of authenticity rages not so much over whether Van Somers did the painting or not. But it is the source of the controversy is as to **who** the portrait shows. It is indeed a truthful likeness of Sir George Somers, or is it not?

The Bermuda Historical Society is repeated on record as being adamently convinced that the person in the portrait is Sir George Somers. By reason of perpetual association and storage, the companion picture is therefore almost certainly that of his wife, Lady Somers.

But there is a well-researched counter-argument to this claim. A position is taken by some that the Van Somers portrait is pure speculation and fantasy, at the very best; that the artist himself never even saw his subject. It is argued that there are so many technical flaws in the picture as to make it virtually worthless as an accurate image of the true Sir George Somers.

A leading proponent of this school of thought is the eminent Bermudian sculptor Desmond Hale Fountain.

In 1982, he was commissioned to begin work on an heroic-size statue of Sir George Somers. The sculptor subsequently set about the task of trying to decide on the stance and form which his statue should take. At the same time he began to contemplate his subject's face and expression. But the more he researched and thought about Sir George Somers appearance, the more he found his evidence to be at odds with that provided by the Van Somers portrait. By 1983, he was openly denying that the painting was anything more than a reasonably well-executed picture of a gentleman from the **second** half of the seventeenth century. He was particularly troubled by the mixed styles of clothing.

Fountain rests his case on several scrupulously documented

facts, each supported by undeniable evidence from various recognised archives, alongside the confirmed opinions of some of the leading authorities in the field.

In specific terms of Sir George's apparent appearance, as given in the Van Somers portrait, the sculptor is completely at odds. He argues that the shape and complexion of the face are more typical of Spanish and Mediterranean types; likewise, the length of hair and style of moustache did not come into fashion in England until many decades after Sir George had died. He challenges the clothing which the portrait shows and pronounces that "every single element of his clothing did not exist in that period, in that combination" and states that none of the "items matches-up within a twenty-five year period either way of his entire life!"

Desmond Fountain argues his stance from a podium populated by a team of international authorities.

A spokesman for the Manchester Gallery of English Costume remarks that ". . . the date that you give, 1609, for the shipwreck of Sir George Somers does not correspond with the type of dress worn in the portrait . . . which in mid-seventeenth century . . ." The Museum of Costume, in Bath, England adds: ". . . his hair is too long for the date of 1609; it really dates from a later period . . ." And world famous author J. L. Nevinson, himself an eminent authority on period clothing, remarks: " . . . I have never seen a 'night gown' with the diagonal striped effect shown in the Paul van Somer portrait, and for style I would have dated it well into the seventeenth century . . ."

But probably the most damning observations are those stated by Diana de Marley, an expert with the respected Courtauld's Institute of London. After noting that the ship depicted in the portrait is quite out of date with anything afloat in Sir George's lifetime, she concludes that "the image of Sir George is all a posthumous concoction!"

Actually, the portrait itself is undated and few people would have problems in accepting that it probably was indeed a posthumous work of art. Certainly this would also conveniently help to explain why the picture portending to be that of Lady Somers actually shows a lady some twenty years different in age to Sir George—when in reality they were very much closer than that. If it is the case that Van Somers painted from hearsay, rather than from a direct sitting, then many of the contradictions over clothing and hair fashions which deeply troubled sculptor Desmond Fountain, are at least explained.

But if the portrait by Van Somers is not a particularly accurate picture of Sir George, then we are still left with the nagging question: What did he actually look like? Unless another verifiable painting is put forth, then we do find ourselves drifting in the realm of reasoned conjecture.

Commencing with his hair, it is indeed possible to speculate as to what this may have looked like. Although trends did tend to dictate that the hair should be either bobbed or close-cut just above the collar-line, there were certainly long-haired exceptions. A portrait of the Earl of Southampton by John Critz the Elder, and dated 1601-3, shows the subject with long black hair which flows neatly over the shoulders. This, however, does depict the gentleman whilst he was imprisoned in The Tower of London and perhaps, therefore, separated from his barber! On the other hand, another portrait confirmed as being the same good Earl presents him with some form of long pony-tail gently draped across his left shoulder—an effeminate taste for fashion which spread into love-knots around his waist, and which was accepted by his contemporaries as being peculiar to the man himself! Literary historian Martin W. Fido describes him as being a "rather silly young peer, who seemed to be making the least of the opportunities his birth offered him . . . "

Another long-haired exception of the period was Christopher Marlowe. A portrait believed to depict this gentleman in the late 1580's also has him with long hair bouncing off his collar, full and feathery.

But such hair-styles were undoubtedly quite unusual in the days of Sir George Somers and, in the absence of any evidence that he himself was inclined towards similar eccentricities, we can safely conclude that he sported a more conventional hairdo, the sort which dropped in an even length and stopped just shy of the top of his collar. In the matter of beards, we do know that they were widely popular—shaving in those days which preceded the development of the safety razor, was doubtless a tiresome and impractical chore. Among men of his own generation, the traditional long, flowing beards were out of favour and most wore a shorter, trimmed beard, or had a moustache with a goatee. We have nothing to indicate that Sir George might have been different from the norms of his day—and therefore assume, with some degree of confidence, that he likewise had some type of goatee and moustache.

With similar conviction, we can also presume that he probably stood about 5 feet six inches tall. Much evidence has been gathered throughout English history to present reasonably accurate estimates of people's heights throughout the ages. Such research focuses not just on unearthed skeletons or preserved corpses, but also on dietetic contents likely to influence growth; architectural evidence regarding heights of doors, ceilings and the such is also useful. A seaman's career had doubtless also endowed him with a slightly more muscular frame than his land-based friends—arms and legs accustomed to pacing decks, climbing steps and rails, and hoisting heavy ropes. His stamina implies that he remained remarkably fit, particularly if we accept his relentless efforts during the three days which preceded the final shipwrecking off Bermuda the year before his death.

Hair styles, beards, height and general physique we can establish with a certain amount of accuracy, based on traditional modes of fashion and habit. We can also use circumstantial evidence to verify that there was nothing abnormal about his general appearance or bearing, for such peculiarities were invariably highlighted by the candid and often disrespectful social circles in which he moved. (Even the highly-regarded Royal favourite Sir Robert Cecil was not immune to such taunting, for a slight spinal disformity resulted in his being openly called "Gobbo," by the Earl of Essex—Italian for "hunchback!")

Finally, we inevitably return to his face: What was that really like? Certainly he must have begun to show signs of being more aged than at the time depicted in the Van Somers portrait. A life of demanding experiences and worries must have literally etched lines across his face, accentuating the corners of his eyes and mouth. His complexion would have been ruddied through continuous exposure to the elements, obliterating any suggestions of the smooth texture and dour colouring which the portrait indicates he may once have had. And he must have had eyes which were full of expression, capable of carrying commands and respect when words were impossible to hear. They must have been alert, responsive; active eyes that moved, darted, reacted.

But again we are in the realm of pure conjecture.

It is at this point that we must turn to the most recent portrait of Sir George Somers—the three-dimensional sculpture created by Desmond Fountain. It is in this contemporary piece of work that we may indeed find a close resemblance to Sir George Somers; a snapshot, if you will, of the man at that singular and precise moment when he emerged from three hopeless days of struggle and despair . . . and suddenly sighted Bermuda.

The statue is slightly larger-than-life and shows the figure of a man with arms open and fingers outstretched, cloak billowing in the wind as disbelief and relief begin to spread across his face.

After contacting some sixty world authorities directly, as well as consulting hundreds of costume and fashion books, the sculptor is confident of the accuracy of the total person he presents.

"The statue is made in heroic scale, which means that it is slightly bigger than he would have been in real life. But I am convinced that this is really what Sir George Somers would have looked like. I have shortened his hair into the more contemporary style of the period and he has been given the correct costume, down to the finest of details. Those clothes he could actually have worn—he is quite English now. It is essential that a long-lasting statue should portray everything as accurately as possible; it must eliminate all erroneous detail because it might very well stand for hundreds of years.

"The people of his day were not particularly tall," he continues, "but I have given him a slightly heavier build than was probably usual. This would be more characteristic of a sixty year-old man who had also enjoyed a certain amount of the excesses of a fairly wealthy life. I think that he would have been quite heavy set."

With regards to the face, he remarks that should the Van Somers portrait bear any likeness at all to the real person, then there are certain physical characteristics which would remain constant, irrespective of hair and costume.

"I have taken the physical structure of the face in the painting," he says, "and **aged** it to the correct age of Sir George Somers in 1609. To this, I have then added the characteristic lines of weathering which seafarers would have had—creases and wrinkles around the eyes, nose and mouth.

"In getting this likeness," he continues, "I have looked at all of the evidence of the period and presented him as a man who also reveals the essential aspects of his character. He was a practical man who wouldn't have appeared on deck in bejewelled Court Dress, in a hurricane! There were very chilling effects of the storm and he would have dressed for it. He most likely would have owned the type of Monmouth Cap I have placed on his head and if he didn't then it would have been in keeping for him to have borrowed one from someone down below deck. He needed to be warm during those three days before the shipwreck. He would not have been wearing sea-boots; these would have become saturated and unbearable after three days, even dangerous and slippery. Therefore I have him wearing a popular type of shoe, which would have been so much more manageable in those conditions."

It has been argued that a person as practical as Sir George Somers unquestionably appears to have been, would hardly have carried-on wearing his sword and a restricting doublet jacket. But Fountain once more responds with conviction:

"This was a man of rank and bearing and he would not have even considered any apparent inconveniences of that sort. He would not have appeared "in public"—even in a storm—without being properly dressed. The loosened, open collar which I have given him would have been the extent to which he might have relaxed in his dress. It was his habit to wear sword and doublet. It must also be remembered that these were days long before sailors had uniforms and badges to show their ranks; even his crew would have been surprised to have seen him on deck without being properly dressed!"

The Desmond Hale Fountain statue stands in Bermuda's original capital, St. George. It was unveiled by Her Royal Highness the Princess Margaret, sister of Her Majesty Queen Elizabeth II. The ceremony, held in October of 1984, served to also commemorate the passing of 375 years since the time of the shipwreck of the "Sea Venture."

* * * * * *

But perhaps the final words should best be from those who knew and sailed with him.

William Strachey described Sir George Somers as being a diligent man, one who was very industrious, meticulous and precise about everything which he did. He admired his dignity and noble bearing and was always saying how justified he considered Sir George's reputation as a seaman to have been. He noted that he was well-liked and affable, a person who was ideal as a mediator in times of stress. He had tact and a becalming nature.

Silvester Jourdain, who perhaps knew him far better, after a lifetime of association with Sir George, seems to totally agree that this was "a gentleman of approved assuredness and ready knowledge of seafaring actions."

These were certainly the talents and qualities which, in themselves, were this remarkable man.

Epilogue

Many people, places and things touched upon the life of Sir George Somers: they were numerous and diverse. Some lingered and others merely drifted across his path and then slipped away.

* * * * * *

Joane Somers—she remarried a year after Sir George was buried. Her second husband was William Raymond of Sussex. They too were childless. She died on 29th. September 1617.

Matthew Somers—upon the death of his first wife, he remarried—this time to Dorothy Hayne. His only daughter Elizabeth became his heir and the Somers estates subsequently passed into the family of John Breare, whom she married. In later life, Matthew became a drunkard. He died in 1625, having suffered a term in prison for debt.

Nicholas Somers—he married and had at least three children, one of whom he named George, in memory of his uncle.

John Somers—he continued to lead a healthy and successful life and became a grandfather many times over. He died on July 12th. 1625, the last survivor of Sir George Somers brothers.

* * * * * *

Sir Walter Raleigh—he remained imprisoned until being released from The Tower on 25th. March 1616. The following year he finally led his expedition to Guiana, but it was a disaster. His son was killed by the Spanish in a raid led by Captain Keymis. The latter committed suicide. Sir Walter returned to England amidst failure and was beheaded on October 29th. that same year.

Captain John Smith—he devoted his energies to writing and proposed that settlements in New England be paired with counterparts in Old England. In 1615, he was imprisoned by French pirates. In England he again met-up briefly with John Rolfe of Virginia. He tried to join the Pilgrim Fathers in 1620, but was rejected. He died in London in June 1631.

Ferdinando Gorges—this Somerset seaman was knighted for his work in developing various schemes relating to the colonisation of the New England area. In 1639 he established a provisional government in Maine. He died in 1647.

Sir Richard Hawkins—he accomplished a circumnavigation which lasted from 1593 until 1602, interrupted by extensive spells in Spanish prisons. He returned a hero, was knighted but then fell into hard times. In 1608 he was arrested for condoning piracy! His last voyage in 1620 was a failed attack against the Barbary Coast with Sir Robert Mansell. He died April 18th. 1622.

Sir James Lancaster—a merchant adventurer who often served in the same fleets as Sir George Somers, he made numerous voyages to India, the Arctic and the Orient. He was born in 1554, the same year as Sir George, and died in London on 6th. June 1618.

* * * * * *

William Strachey—he finally left Virginia and returned to the literary circles of London, where he had a minor reputation as a critic. He died on 21st. June 1621 and was buried in St. Giles Church, Camberwell.

Silvester Jourdain—after returning to England, he enjoyed much attention for his booklet on the events of the Bermuda shipwreck. His account was reprinted several times soon after. He died in 1650 and was buried in St. Sepulchre Church, Newgate.

John Rolfe—he settled contentedly in Virginia and was perhaps the first colonist to actually make commercial profit from the growing of tobacco. He married Pocahontas, the legendary Indian Princess who subsequently enjoyed considerable popularity in the Court of King James.

George Yeardley—he had originally been aboard "Sea Venture" as commander of the land forces under Sir Thomas Gates. He was knighted and twice served terms as Governor of Virginia.

Stephen Hopkins—generally branded as having been troublesome in Bermuda during the period when the "Deliverance" and "Patience" were being built, he eventually returned to England—only to make a second voyage to Virginia, as one of the original Pilgrim Fathers in 1620.

Reverend Richard Bucke—he continued to serve as Chaplain to the Virginia Company. He remained in Virginia and officiated at the John Rolfe/Pocahontas wedding. He died there in 1623 and a plaque in his memory was erected in Wymondham Abbey, Norfolk, England where he was born, by his American descendents in 1977.

Christopher Carter—reputedly never left Bermuda again. He decided to remain after the first settlers arrived; entered local politics and married. He died many years later in an accident.

* * * * * *

Sir Henry Wriothesley, (Earl of Southampton)—his life continued to fluctuate between heroics in battle and bouts of social irresponsibility. In 1621, he was arrested for "mischevious intrigues" following a fight in public with the Duke of Buckingham. In 1624 he went to Holland as commander of a Troop; his son died in battle and Henry died on the return trip from "lethargy," on 10th. November.

Sir Thomas Smith—he was replaced as Treasurer of the Virginia in 1618, a position then assumed by Edwin Sandys. He died in 1625.

Philip Herbert—removed from the Royal Staff after fighting in the House of Lords with Lord Mountjoy, in May 1641. He joined the ranks of the anti-Royalists in the Civil War, became a Member of Parliament and died on 23rd. January 1650.

William Herbert—continued serving in various public offices until dying in 1630, whilst Chancellor of Oxford. His mother Mary, forever a patron of the Arts, died on 25th. September 1621.

Lucy Harrington—an Elizabethan patron of The Arts, she was widowed in 1627 and her extensive wealth continued to be offered to various writers and poets. She invested heavily in the Virginia Company.

Richard Hakluyt—in 1612 he became a Charter Member of the North-West Passage Company, whilst continuing to serve as an advisor to various other seafaring ventures. He died at the age of 64 on 23rd. November 1616.

William Shakespeare—a few months after the burial of Sir George Somers, "The Tempest" was first performed in London (November 1st. 1611). It was based on the 1609 shipwreck of Sir George Somers—a man he had often met socially. The playwright died in 1616; his wife, Anne Hathaway, died in 1623.

* * * * * *

Sir Thomas Gates and **Captain Christopher Newport** both continued with successful life-long careers as seamen, administrators and colonisers. The fate of **"Patience"** and **"Deliverance"** remains something of a mystery. Although there was a vessel named "Patience" registered in Lyme Regis in about 1614, this was probably not the same one which brought back Sir George Somers for burial.

Whitchurch Canonicorum remains a tiny hamlet nestled contentedly among narrow lanes and "weys"; its church contains a plaque commemorating the life of this man who had sat in its pews on Sundays; **Berne Manor** was gutted by a fire at the start of the twentieth century, but has been restored. On Sunday 31st. July 1983, one of the original flagstones from the central hallway was carried to Bermuda by Bob Burns, St. George's town-crier—a permanent momento of the links between both places.

* * * * * *

Bermuda celebrated the 375th. Anniversary of Sir George Somers' shipwreck, in 1984, having evolved into one of the most attractive vacation resorts in the Western Hemisphere. The actual wreck of the **"Sea Venture"** was discovered in October 1958 by Edmund Downing–appropriately enough he was not only a Virginian, but also a direct descendent of Sir George Yeardley, one of the passengers aboard the boat when it was wedged in that same spot in 1609.

Virginia thrived and the tobacco crop which John Rolfe had once begun became the base for its economy and international fame. As an historical focal-point for the United States of America, the original former colony remains the key to much of the country's history.

Lyme Regis eventually diminished in importance as a port and by the twentieth century had become a seaside resort catering to holiday-makers—a place where they might relax, go fishing or just amble through its attractive, narrow streets. Enjoying, in fact, many of those same things which one of the town's most famous sons had . . . four hundred years before.

* * * * * *

Sir George Somers [sketch by Branhill—1881].

The Cobb, Lyme Regis.

Richard Austin

St. Michael's Church, Lyme Regis.

The Guild Hall, Lyme Regis.

Richard Austin

Fish pots and buildings along The Cobb, Lyme Regis.

Broad Street, Lyme Regis—today.

Modern-day Lyme Regis—the town centre.

Berne Manor in Dorset, England.

Elizabeth I, Queen of England.

Mary I, Queen of England.

Sir Walter Raleigh.

Sir Francis Walsingham.

Sir Henry Wriothesley, Earl of Southampton.

Sir Robert Devereaux, Earl of Essex.

Sir Philip Herbert, Earl of Montgomery.

Sir William Herbert, Earl of Pembroke.

The shipwreck of "Sea Venture" in 1609—an artist's impression.

Replica of "Deliverance" in St. George, Bermuda.

The Cobb steps [left] up which Sir George Somers' body was carried after its return from Bermuda.

Gravestones and main entrance to St. Wita's Church, Dorset.

The Church of St. Wita at Whitchurch Canonicorum, Dorset.

IN MEMORY OF THE COLONISER OF THE BERMUDAS

Memorial plaque to Sir George Somers—twin plaques are in England and Bermuda.

The tomb marking the site of Sir George's heart, in Bermuda.

Memorial obelisk in Somers Garden, Bermuda.

1609 - 1909

IN COMMEMORATION OF THE
SETTLEMENT OF THESE ISLANDS
ON THE 28TH OF JULY 1609
AND
IN HONOUR OF ADMIRAL
SIR GEORGE SOMERS KT.
AT WHOSE INSTANCE LARGELY
THE SETTLEMENT WAS EFFECTED
THIS MEMORIAL
HAS BEEN ERECTED OUT OF A
GRANT MADE BY THE LEGISLATURE
OF THIS COLONY

Commemorative plaque to Sir George Somers in Bermuda.

Index

-186-

COMMENTS AND REVIEWS:

❦❦❦❦❦❦❦❦❦

" . . . fascinating and well-written . . . deserves attention . . . "
James Goodsell, 'Christian Science Monitor' - U.S.A.

♦ ♦ ♦ ♦

" . . . colourful and useful . . . has clearly dug deeply . . . "
'Western morning News' - ENGLAND.

♦ ♦ ♦ ♦

" . . . extensive research . . . very interesting and well presented . . . "
'The Sun' - BERMUDA.

♦ ♦ ♦ ♦

" . . . excellent book . . . valuable addition to our library . . . "
Tom Mor, 'New World Tapestry' - ENGLAND.

♦ ♦ ♦ ♦

" . . . solidly researched . . . imaginative . . . "
'Royal Gazette' - BERMUDA.

♦ ♦ ♦ ♦

" . . . impressed with the amount of research . . . "
J.N.H., Historian to Department of the Interior - U.S.A.

♦ ♦ ♦ ♦

" . . . follows Sir George's whole career, bringing out many
sidelights which may surprise the reader . . . "
'Bulletin of the Institute of Maritime History and Archaeology'

♦ ♦ ♦ ♦